# The Journey Starts Here:
# Global Management
# And
# Tourism Trends

# The Journey Starts Here: Global Management And Tourism Trends

## Dr. Adyasha Das

BLACK EAGLE BOOKS
2020

BLACK EAGLE BOOKS

USA address:
7464 Wisdom Lane
Dublin, OH 43016

India address:
E/312, Trident Galaxy, Kalinga Nagar,
Bhubaneswar-751003, Odisha, India

E-mail: info@blackeaglebooks.org
Website: www.blackeaglebooks.org

First International Edition published by
Black Eagle Books, 2020

**The Journey Starts Here: Global Management And Tourism Trends by Dr. Adyasha Das**

Copyright © **Dr. Adyasha Das**

All rights reserved. No part of this publication may be reproduced, stored in a retrieval system, or transmitted, in any form or by any means, electronic, mechanical, photocopying, recording or otherwise without the prior permission of the publisher.

Interior Design: Ezy's Publication

ISBN- 978-1-64560-063-3 (Paperback)
Library of Congress Control Number: 2020932537

Printed in United States of America

# CONTENTS

| | |
|---|---:|
| Non-Religious Religious Tourism | 11 |
| Identifying Primary Areas Of Government Mal-Functioning In Naxal Affected Districts Of Odisha | 29 |
| Backpacking Travel Culture: Reflections Of Indonesia | 48 |
| Civic Governance: Aesthetics And Amenities- Destination Odisha | 62 |
| The Impact Of Ethical Policing | 74 |
| Medical Tourism: A New Horizon | 84 |
| Identity Tourism | 92 |
| Mind And Music | 106 |
| Music Tourism : The Innovative Edge | 114 |
| Issues In Inclusive Organisational Dynamics | 125 |
| Sufism As A Way Of Life | 141 |
| From Self To Self: Sufism And Transcultural Expressions | 155 |
| Tourism Marketing : Global Trends | 169 |
| Impacts Of Tourism Development | 175 |
| Festival Tourism And Culture | 197 |

# Preface

In recent times, the tourism and hospitality industry has undergone a metamorphosis , marked by increasing competitiveness and a dynamic market. The nature of demand has changed along with the profile of the consumer. Organizational success, thus, depends greatly on the efficient management of service provision and delivery.

Learning and innovation are prerequisites for sustainable tourism in a transnational environment. Making available innovative and redefined tourism products is extremely important for tourism regions. There is universal acceptance of the need for innovation in tourism, i.e. creating additional, commercially relevant value through the redesign of products, processes, management, logistics, and/or collaborative and regulatory structures. A number of bottle-necks can be identified, of which quite a few relate to human resource practices and the sector's organizational structure. In particular, lack of sensible ways to retain employees, training and succession planning challenge the sustainability of the sector's many small and medium sized tourism enterprises . Along with this, lack of trust and fear of change constitute major barriers to the generation and use of knowledge to nourish innovation in tourism.

Greater appreciation of leisure time, urbanization, the ageing of the population, climate change and the noticeable trend towards individualism are among the challenges to which tourism must find new, innovative solutions. Silence and cleanliness will represent a luxury in the future, but how can we benefit from these commercially? Tourism competes for consumers' leisure time with many other industries. Globalization is progressing rapidly, challenging industrial and economic structures. It is acknowledged that increased innovation is the key to responding to this challenge. Supporting tourism innovations will provide an opportunity to create new tourism markets and reinvent old ones. The tourism industry is changing, driven notably by new consumer requirements and information technologies. A new tourism is emerging - one which takes into account the complexity and segmentation of tourism demand, the greater flexibility of supply, distribution and consumption and the search for new sources of profitability in the industry. Tourism entrepreneurs have realized that innovation is becoming a key element to survive and compete in a dynamic and radically changing environment.

Innovation is at the core of creating a sustainable human society. Innovation is critical for the on-going success of any enterprise. Organizations that do not innovate disappear. Innovation is a necessary but not sufficient ingredient for sustainable growth. This is because innovations are often not specifically directed at sustainable growth, which in turn can be attributed to the differences in goals between industry and society. However, new innovations turn into sustainable business assets only if they are acceptable to society at large.

Within the field of tourism, innovation is generally seen to be far behind other industries. Tourism is largely characterized by being directed at satisfying consumer needs, increasing market share and competitiveness rather than the reduction of environmental impacts. The challenge of integrating sustainability thinking into business processes is significant, but if not successfully met will not be sustainable. Innovation can lead to more business value if the business pursues a path to sustainable development and incorporates the issues of sustainability into its development process.

Innovation is essential for sustainable development of tourism. However, within tourism it is also problematic in three ways. First, it is often seen as defective or lagging far behind most other industries. Second, innovation is often not directed at reducing environmental impacts but at satisfying customer needs, increasing market share and competitiveness Third, tourism products are the result of complicated multi-sector networks. This means that many innovations in tourism are induced by innovations from supplying sectors like transportation and communication.

This book is a collection of articles on various trends that are influencing the dynamics of the Tourism and Travel industry. A new tourism is emerging - one which takes into account the complexity and segmentation of tourism demand, the greater flexibility of supply, distribution and consumption and the search for new sources of profitability in the industry. Innovation is a crucial driver to develop and establish successful, dynamic, customer-centric e-tourism platforms. The competitiveness and sustainable growth of the tourism sector in its economic, social and cultural dimensions is impossible without innovations. Globalization is progressing rapidly, challenging industrial and economic structures. It is acknowledged that increased innovation is the key to responding to this challenge. Supporting tourism innovations will provide an opportunity enabling emerging destinations to create new tourism markets and reinvent old ones. Success in the global economy is increasingly determined by a firm's ability to respond innovatively to the changing views and needs of customers– the demand-side of the market.

# NON-RELIGIOUS RELIGIOUS TOURISM

In preparation of a study of Western visitors to the holy city of Puri, the purpose of this paper is to conduct a literature review on cultural tourism to religious sites, based on that, to identify lines of research. In the last three decades, a respectable amount of scholarly literature has been published on religious tourism. Most of the literature is concerned with either the tourists affiliated with the religion in question, i.e. tourists with a religious motive behind the tourism, or the management of such tourists. Secular or cultural tourists for whom sites and activities of other persons' religion is an attraction, is relatively less researched.

In the literature review it is found that research to do with secular/cultural visitors to sites of others' religion predominantly is about sites with physical manifestations of religious activities (temples, architecture), while research on visitors witnessing other persons' religious practices (pilgrimages, gatherings, ceremonies, rituals etc.) is rather sparse. Management of sites and conflict avoidance, ensuring the needs of religious practitioners while maintaining the attractiveness of the site for the secular visitor, is a recurring topic in the research. The reason for this might be found in the Western-centric intellectual history of tourism research. Even so, the literature review finds that surprisingly little is known about the background and causes of visits by international visitors not belonging to the faith of the religious site or event in question. Based on the findings in the literature review, promising lines of research are identified, to do with perceived authenticity, secular pilgrimage, and spiritual dimensions in post-secular tourism, which all invite an emic approach to the research.Introduction

Ever since Turner and Turner's oft quoted (and at the time of publication rather contentious) statement that "(…) a tourist is half a pilgrim, if a pilgrim is half a tourist(…)" (Turner & Turner, 1978: 20), the interlinkage between tourism and pilgrimage has been recognised, researched, and discussed. In 1992, in her introduction to a groundbreaking special issue of *Annals of Tourism Research*, Smith summed up the relation between pilgrimage and tourism by means of a continuum with sacred and secular designating the extreme positions of the continuum, on which pious pilgrims were located at the 'sacred' end, secular tourists located at the 'secular' end, and different versions of 'religious tourism' located in the middle, with various degrees of balance between pilgrimage and tourism determining the actual location on the continuum (Smith, 1992: 4). That same year, another groundbreaking publication appeared, Morinis' edited book on the anthropology of pilgrimage (Morinis, 1992). In a chapter in this publication, Cohen (1992) argued that the divergence between tourism and pilgrimage could be viewed by means of the contrast between the quest for the center (pilgrimage), and the search for the other (tourism). However, Cohen also argued that there are strong convergences between pilgrimage and tourism, thus also supporting Turner & Turner's (1978) initial viewpoint.

A few years ago, Olsen (2010: 848) argued that this "pilgrim-tourist dichotomy [is] probably the most debated topic relating to religion and tourism in the literature today." The authors of this paper agree with Olsen on this, yet we would additionally argue that the focus on the overlap between tourism in pilgrimage and pilgrimage in tourism may unwittingly have restrained the perspective to one of 'more or less (pilgrim/tourist).'We argue that, in order to understand more deeply the tourism activities at religious sites and thus enabling a better management, it is necessary to acknowledge that religious tourists need not themselves have any religious, spiritual or faithwise connection to the religion in question, but may perceive the religious activities or structures at the location visited as something of *cultural* rather than religious interest. Other visitors, while harbouring spiritual reasons for a visit to a location of religious importance, may not at all be connected to the religion of that location.

The above contemplations were brought home to us as part of initial research on Western visitors to the holy city of Puri. Since the 1970's and the days of the hippie travellers, there has been a small but steady trickle of self-organised, independent tourists coming to Puri. At its height, it had a reasonably well-developed commercial service-infrastructure, with hotels, guesthouses, restaurants travel agents and an informal economy servicing the Western hippie-travellers and their backpacker successors(Sørensen & Babu, 2008). Yet, at the same time, Puri is a location where, unlike for instance Varanasi, the religious practices of the Hindu pilgrims are not continuously conspicuously visible for the Western outsider, and at the same time Puri is also a location of domestic tourism of a character where religious motives may wary, from the intense devotion, over the superficially religious, to the secular visits for recreational purposes.

Puri, in this way, encapsulates the multifaceted realities of visits to sites of religious importance, and it amply demonstrates the need for tourism scholars to develop knowledge in a decidedly ecclectic manner, pursuing both empirical knowledge on religiously motivated travel, as well as conceptual developments in comprehending the many dimensions of tourism practices at locations of religious importance. Yet, a first step in pursuing such research ambitions is to take stock of extant scholarly research, in order to assess the character and quality of knowledge on the cultural tourism visitors to sites of religious importance.

In the following, therefore, we present the results of an ambitious review of scholarly research on cultural (non-religious) tourism to sites of religious activities. We do this through a perusing of extant literature on the subject. In this, we introduce the predominant themes of research evident in the literature, and we tentatively consider the research lacunae. Through the latter we identify promising avenues of future research, having the ambition to expand the view of religious tourism and the management of this to encompass the non-religious (and often economically attractive) visitors. While not claiming to be exhaustive, we contend that the review is thorough, and thus that it serves as a robust platform, from which to pursue research in the impact and management of non-religious visitors to sites of religious importance.

Few, if any countries are so richly endowed as India, in terms of opportunities to study this, given the multitude of faiths and religious sited that entices both religious and secular travel. As will be evident in the following, confronting extant research with the case of India also reveals clear Euro-centric biases of perspectives, and thus also illuminate a need for a more conspicuous Indian scholarly presence in the international scientific debate on the matter. However, the flip-side of this point obviously points to the need of discussing the merits and demerits of drawing together such research irrespective on the faiths that are involved. This is a neccessay discussion, yet one that can only be hinted at in this paper.

### Literature review

The extant literature is somewhat limited in extent.In the following, it has been chosen to focus the literature review on four issues, two to do with sites and management respectively, and two to do with conceptualisation of non-religious visitors and the visitor impetus respectively.

### Conceptualising non-religious religious tourists

A key issue in the little literature that exists on the issue is that fuzziness of distinguishing between the religious and the non-religious in visits to religious sites. Arguably, non-religious tourism presence at religious sites cannot be conceptualised independently of the religiously motivated presence. In order to understand the similarities and differences between the various visitors to a religious site, it is necessary to take point of departure in what draws people to the location. This seems to be the tacit starting point in the literature. Therefore, some sort of conception of what is religious tourism is necessary in order to comprehend what tourism at religious sites is not religious tourism.

Rinschede defines religious tourism as "that type of

tourism whose participants are motivated in part or exclusively for religious reasons" (1992: 52), with a focus on the participants. Statistically, however, it seems that all visitors to a religious site are viewed as religious tourists. The site, not the motivation, seems to be the determining issue, thus including all visitors to a religious site in the category of religious tourism.

Shinde and Rizello (2014) explore the fuzzy boundary between religious and non-religious tourism in their study of weekend visitors to two religious sites: Vrindavan in India, and the Shrine of Santimissa Medici in Italy. They find that, while such weekend visitors do not fit into a pilgrim-tourist continuum, on the whole the religious motive is the main driver.

In her seminal work on the management of sacred sites, Shackley (2001a) distinguish between visitors who are there for a religious experience, and visitors who have come to visit religious heritage. Griffiths (2011: 65), however, argue that a third type must be recognised, namely the visitor whose motivation derives from architectural reasons or other features.

There is more to it than that, however. Collins-Kreiner (2010) argues that it is not only a matter of distinguishing between religious pilgrimage and secular tourism: visits to religious buildings may be non-religious, yet still carry the characteristics of pilgrimage. Collins-Kreiner describes the conceptual conundrum this way:

"But how does one distinguish a visitor on a genuine quest forprayer and spiritual peace from one admiring the work of 11th or 12$^{th}$century builders, or another contemplating the tomb of a famous person?A key issue (…) relates to the existence of a continuumamong different types of visitors - not arranged in accordance withtheir description as pilgrims or tourists, as in Smith (1992), but inaccordance with the visit's effect on the visitors themselves. Tourism literaturetypically pays a great deal of attention to the effect of tourismon the local population and relatively little attention to the effect onthe visitors themselves (duration, strength, and level)." (Collins-Kreiner, 2010: 451)

In her study of visitors to the Roman Catholic church of La Sagrada Familia in Barcelona, Spain, Marine-Roig(2015) points to the same conceptual challenge, namely that 'pilgrimage' need not be religious. Thus, the many visitors to La Sagrada Familia who comes to admire the unique architectural style of the architect Antonio Gaudi, can be viewed as pilgrims, for whom the church is not visited for religious purposes, yet nevertheless serves as pilgrimage location for such visitors.

In another study of the same location, La Sagrada Familia, Barcelone, Spain, Nilsson and Tesfahuney(2016) relates this same issue of non-religious pilgrimages to the emerging tourism research debate on 'the post-secular' pilgrimage tourism, thus adding an additional dimension of complexity to the understanding.

A final twist to the matter of conceptualisation consists in the fact that not all in a travel party to a religious site necessarily share the same motivations. Abbate & Nuovo studied the relationships between personality traits and motivations for religious travel. The results indicated that motivation is focused prevalently on the need for discovery in men and socialisation in women (Abbate & Di Nuovo, 2013).

In summary, no clear conceptualisation has yet emerged from the research literature. Any desires to work with simple either/or typology is challenged by the multidimensional overlaps of motivations, relations, and changing societal and religious conditions in which any conceptualisation necessarily is embedded.

## Types of religious sites present in research

Our extensive readings suggest to usthat research to do with secular/cultural visitors to sites of others' religion predominantly is about sites with physical manifestations of religious activities, such as temples, mosques, churches or other structures of religious significance.Research on visitors witnessing other persons' religious practices (pilgrimages, gatherings, ceremonies, rituals etc.) is rather sparse in comparison.

This tallies well with the observation of Rivera et al that 88 percent of all World Heritage Sites have religioussignificance(Rivera, Shani, & Severt, 2009) since sites of religioustraditions commonly attract large numbers of visitors. The Ganges River, StPeter's Basilica, the Salt Lake Temple, Borobudur and Prambanan,Angkor Wat, Old Jerusalem, the Taj Mahal and the Baha'i Gardensare world-class examples of attractions for religious and seculartourists(Collins-Kreiner & Gatrell, 2006; Olsen, 2012; Shackley, 2001a, 2001b; K. Shinde, 2012).

The religiously affiliated structures that are present in extant research is not limited to World Heritage buildings, however. Also natural structures like the abovementioned Ganges River, orUluru (Ayers Rock) in Australia (Digance, 2003)is present in the research, as is buildings of less international fame, such as cathedrals in Victoria, Australia (Griffiths, 2011)and churches in Helsinki, Finland (Jokela, 2013).

Compared to that, research on visitors witnessing other persons' religious practices (pilgrimages, gatherings, ceremonies, rituals etc.) is somewhat sparse. Yet, it is present in the tourism research tradition in which the focus is on sociocultural impacts. Notably, however, the research in this tradition seems to subsume religious activities under the concept of culture. An interesting example of such research is Hernandez-Ramdwar's study of African traditional religions in the Caribbean and South America as a tourist attraction and the impacts and commodification that it has had (Hernandez-Ramdwar, 2013).

### Site and visitor management

Much of the extant literature on the non-religious visitors to religious sites is about management of sites and visitors. In fact, it is such writings that the issue of the non-religious visitor to religious sites most often crops up at all. Issues include, but are not limited to, management of sites and managerial viewpoints(Ballantyne, Hughes, & Bond, 2016), conflicts and conflict avoidance between religious and non-religious users (Bloch, 2017; Digance, 2003; Kasim, 2011), religious visitors' view of non-religious visitation and disturbance(Griffiths, 2011), facilitation and interpretation for the non-religious visitors(Hughes, Bond, & Ballantyne, 2013).

The underlying *raison* d'etre for this line of research can be described as the challenge of ensuring the needs of religious practitioners while maintaining the attractiveness of the site for the secular visitor. The reason for this might be found in the Western-centric intellectual history of tourism research. This, for instance, can be argued by pointing to the dual role of many cathedrals in Europe as both church for a congregation, and major tourist attractions that the Western-centric research literature contain.

There are other approaches, however. Woodward (2004) discusses the challenges of managing non-religious tourism to sites of world faiths. He points out the salient fact that, for many areas that have a site or sites of religious importance, the income from the non-religious visitors are an important source of revenue for the area, but that faith buildings may have volume challenges and conflict challenges. Buultjens et al (2005), in their study of a Sri Lankan national park pointed out that the management of tourism impact in the park did not recognize the impacts of religious tourism to the park as an issue.

In this way, curiously, Buultjens et al illuminate the underlying lopsidedness of perspective in favour of the religious tourists that can be argued to be present in much research. No wonder in this lopsidedness, of course: in the vast majority of cases, it is the religious rooting of the attraction that has made it into an attraction also for the non-religious visitor, and therefore research on the site management tend to see the non-religious visitors as 'late-comers' and possible intruders. Yet, in the case of the Sri Lankan national park that Buultjens et al study, the non-religious visitors do *not* visit it because of the religious significance, yet it is their impacts on the national park, not the impact of the religious tourism to the park, that is seen as a managerial challenge. In this way Buultjens et al therefore can serve as an illustration of the need for a more multifaceted research on management challenges in connection with sites that are consumed by both religious and non-religious visitor.

### Non-religious visitor impetus

Extant research on the motivation of the non-religious visitor to religious sites is quite limited. Non-religious motivations is *not* absent from the literature, but in most of the literature, the non-religious element consists of an acknowledgement of religious visitors also having more secular (hedonic) tourism motives. Some studies specifically explore the issue of non-religious motivations among religious visitors (Abbate & Di Nuovo, 2013; Knox, Hannam, Margry, Olsen, & Salazar, 2014). But the other side of the coin, the motivation behind the non-religious visit to religious sites, is almost absent from the literature.

In some papers, data on this is presented, with a comparative or conflict-focused perspective, comparing or contrasting data on the religious visitor with other visitors (Digance, 2003; Griffiths, 2011). Nyaupane, Timothy and Poudel (2015) researched visitors to Lumbini (birthplace of Buddha). The visitors were classified in self-identified visitor types. The research shows clear differences between the ones who declare themselves pilgrims and those who declare themselves tourists. From these studies, it is possible to elicit some insights on motivation behind non-religious visits, but the insights are limited by the comparation or contrasting that is the purpose of these papers.

In a few papers, the focus is explicitly on the non-religious visit. For instance Hughes et al (2013)describes secular visitors to Canterbury cathedral, UK, and how they desire better display and signage to do with the non-religious elements, such as architecture and history. More broadly, Jokela argues that religious sites are popular tourist attractions because "they are place-specific landmarks that mediate conceptions about history and identity" (2013: 252).

Summing it up, the the extant research literature is surprisingly limited on knowledge regarding the impetuses behind non-religious visitors to religious sites. Extant research throw some light on reasons for visits to physical manifestations (temples, architecture, churches, building), but is all but absent in terms of visits to religious practices (pilgrimages, gatherings, ceremonies, rituals etc.).

## Discussion

The above literature review has been conducted on the somewhat presumptious condition of *not* separating the findings according to religious faiths of the religious practitioner or religious building or site. We find it justifiable to do so precisely because the point of departure for our research is not any specific religion, instead it is the cultural visitor to a religious site, where the visit is not derived from the person's religion. Scholarly knowledge on such visitors, we argue, may benefit from pooling the insights from cases of different location or religious connection, precisely because the tourists in question are not pursuing religion.

As it is, it seems that other dimensions than actual religions have had more influence on the character of the extant knowledge, and not least that the background of the researchers are massively influential. The research is predominantly Western-centric. This is partly seen in the choice of cases investigated and the religious affiliation of these cases, partly seen in the affiliation of the researchers, but more importantly, it is also seen in the underlying 'take' on the subject of tourism. It is a Western-centric understanding of tourism, based on supposed differentiation between work and leisure, religion and everyday, and home and away, that underpins the perspectives encountered in the research on cultural tourism at religious sites.

The literature review showed that, while the extant literature is somewhat limited on the topic of cultural visitors to religious sites, visitors who are not there for the purpose of carrying out their faith, there is nevertheless a body of published research to build on. In many researches, such visitor are briefly mentioned, and in a few papers, they are at the core of the research. Yet, no clear-cut conceptualisation has gained position. This may signal that no all-comprehensive conceptualisation of the non-faith based tourism to religious sites can or should be aimed for. Maybe it is necessary to utilise ad-hoc conceptualisations in relation to the specific site or religion of site, so as to more thoroughly capture the relation between the religion/religious activity/site and the non-religious visitors. Such an approach would benefit from careful use of the concept of authenticity. Not authenticity in any evaluative sense of the term, but in terms of perceived authenticity or experiental authenticity. Such concepts would help to throw light on the individual and collective meaning of the consumption of religious sites by cultural tourism visitors.

This would also produce insights on non-religious pilgrimages, whether these be viewed as secular or post-secular, and certainly bring additional insights into the spiritual dimensions of post-secular tourism. All this, however, calls for a more *emic* research approach, with more in-depth participatory engagement.

Olsen (2011) convincingly argues that the knowledge on the 'meeting' of tourism and religion to some degree misses out on the religious view of this meeting, in favour of the academic view. Olsen calls for tourism scholars to take more seriously the religious views on tourism, in the location where religion and tourism intersects and overlaps. Olsen's viewpoint can be argued to be a call for a more emic approach to research into tourism to religious sites. More explicitly, the study by Buzinde et al (2014) of Kumbh Mela pilgrimage aim for an emic understanding of the pilgrimage experience. We contend that ambitions for an insider's comprehension, an emic understanding, is equally relevant as regards the non-religious use of religious sites. A key element in this would be ethnographic participant-observation studies of cultural tourism to religious sites. Such studies, incidentally, would also have the potential of providing a better footing for the marketing and management of such sites, inasmuch as it would enlighten us on what, exactly it is that is being marketed and managed – according to the cultural tourism visitor.

## Conclusion

This paper started with the argument that, while it is insightful to view the interrelation between pilgrim and tourist on a 'more-or-less pilgrim-or tourist' continuum, this also entails a risk of overlooking some non-tourist activities at religious sites, which cannot be positioned at this continnum. The literature review enlarged on this and reveled that extant literature on cultural tourism visitors to religious sites is somewhat sparse, and when found, is mostly to do with the management of these in relation to faith-based use of the structures or locations.

No general conceptualisation has emerged from the literature, and indeed it is doubtful if such one would be of general use value. However, the underlying tone of the extant research is, as tourism research in general, very much grounded in a Western-centric understanding of tourism. This is also witnessed in the cases studied in the extant research. India, while being present in the body of literature on the subject, is proportionally vastly underrepresented, not least when taken the amount of religious tourism, including pilgrimages, into account. It is to be hoped that more cases from the Indian subcontinent on the subject of cultural tourism to religious sites will find their way to publication. This will nuance and broaden the scholarly understanding of the subject, empirically as well as theoretically.

Adyasha Das and Anders Sorensen

**References**
- Abbate, C. S., & Di Nuovo, S. (2013). Motivation and personality traits for choosing religious tourism. A research on the case of Medjugorje. *Current Issues in Tourism,* 16(5), 501-506. doi:10.1080/13683500.2012.749844
- Ballantyne, R., Hughes, K., & Bond, N. (2016). Using a Delphi approach to identify managers' preferences for visitor interpretation at Canterbury Cathedral World Heritage Site. *Tourism Management,* 54, 72-80. doi:http://dx.doi.org/10.1016/j.tourman.2015.10.014
- Bloch, N. (2017). Barbarians in India. Tourism as moral contamination. *Annals of Tourism Research,* 62, 64-77. doi:http://dx.doi.org/10.1016/j.annals.2016.12.001
- Buultjens, J., Ratnayake, I., Gnanapala, A., & Aslam, M. (2005). Tourism and its implications for management in Ruhuna National Park (Yala), Sri Lanka. *Tourism Management,* 26(5), 733-742. doi:http://dx.doi.org/10.1016/j.tourman.2004.03.014
- Buzinde, C. N., Kalavar, J. M., Kohli, N., & Manuel-Navarrete, D. (2014). Emic understandings of Kumbh Mela pilgrimage experiences. *Annals of Tourism Research,* 49, 1-18. doi:http://dx.doi.org/10.1016/j.annals.2014.08.001
- Cohen, E. (1992). Pilgrimage and Tourism: Convergence

and divergence. In A. Morinis (Ed.), *Sacred Journeys* (pp. 47-61). London: Greenwood Press.
- Collins-Kreiner, N. (2010). Researching pilgrimage: Continuity and Transformations. *Annals of Tourism Research, 37*(2), 440-456. doi:http://dx.doi.org/10.1016/j.annals.2009.10.016
- Collins-Kreiner, N., & Gatrell, J. D. (2006). Tourism, Heritage and Pilgrimage: The Case of Haifa's Bahá'í Gardens. *Journal of Heritage Tourism, 1*(1), 32-50.
- Digance, J. (2003). Pilgrimage at contested sites. *Annals of Tourism Research, 30*(1), 143-159. doi:http://dx.doi.org/10.1016/S0160-7383(02)00028-2
- Griffiths, M. (2011). Those who come to pray and those who come to look: interactions between visitors and congregations. *Journal of Heritage Tourism, 6*(1), 63-72.
- Hernandez-Ramdwar, C. (2013). African traditional religions in the Caribbean and Brazil: models of religious tourism and impacts of commodification. *Journal of Heritage Tourism, 8*(1), 81-88. doi:10.1080/1743873X.2013.765750
- Hughes, K., Bond, N., & Ballantyne, R. (2013). Designing and managing interpretive experiences at religious sites: Visitors' perceptions of Canterbury Cathedral. *Tourism Management, 36*, 210-220. doi:http://dx.doi.org/10.1016/j.tourman.2012.11.022
- Jokela, S. E. (2013). Tourism and identity politics in the Helsinki churchscape. *Tourism Geographies, 16*(2), 252-269. doi:10.1080/14616688.2013.865070
- Kasim, A. (2011). Balancing Tourism and Religious Experience: Understanding Devotees' Perspectives on Thaipusam in Batu Caves, Selangor, Malaysia. *Journal of Hospitality Marketing & Management, 20*(3-4), 441-456. doi:10.1080/19368623.2011.562437

- Knox, D., Hannam, K., Margry, P. J., Olsen, D. H., & Salazar, N. B. (2014). Is Tourist a Secular Pilgrim or a Hedonist in Search of Pleasure? *Tourism Recreation Research, 39*(2), 235-267. doi:10.1080/02508281.2014.11081769
- Marine-Roig, E. (2015). Religious tourism versus secular pilgrimage: The Basilica of La Sagrada Familia. *International Journal of Religious Tourism and Pilgrimage, 3*(1), 25-37.
- Morinis, A. (Ed.) (1992). *Sacred Journeys: The Anthropology of Pilgrimage*. Westport: Greenwood Press.
- Nilsson, M., & Tesfahuney, M. (2016). Performing the "post-secular" in Santiago de Compostela. *Annals of Tourism Research, 57*, 18-30. doi:http://dx.doi.org/10.1016/j.annals.2015.11.001
- Nyaupane, G. P., Timothy, D. J., & Poudel, S. (2015). Understanding tourists in religious destinations: A social distance perspective. *Tourism Management, 48*, 343-353. doi:http://dx.doi.org/10.1016/j.tourman.2014.12.009
- Olsen, D. H. (2010). Pilgrims, tourists and Max Weber's "ideal types". *Annals of Tourism Research, 37*(3), 848-851. doi:http://dx.doi.org/10.1016/j.annals.2010.02.002
- Olsen, D. H. (2011). Towards a religious view of tourism: negotiating faith perspectives on tourism. *Tourism Culture & Communication, 11*(1), 17-30.
- Olsen, D. H. (2012). Negotiating identity at religious sites: a management perspective. *Journal of Heritage Tourism, 7*(4), 359-366. doi:10.1080/1743873X.2012.722642
- Rinschede, G. (1992). Forms of religious tourism. *Annals of Tourism Research, 19*(1), 51-67. doi:http://dx.doi.org/10.1016/0160-7383(92)90106-Y
- Rivera, M. A., Shani, A., & Severt, D. (2009). Perceptions

- of service attributes in a religious theme site: an importance-satisfaction analysis. *Journal of Heritage Tourism*, 4(3), 227-243.
- Shackley, M. (2001a). *Managing Sacred Sites: Service Provision and Visitor Experience*. London: Continuum.
- Shackley, M. (2001b). Sacred World Heritage Sites: Balancing Meaning With Management. *Tourism Recreation Research*, 26(1), 5-10.
- Shinde, K. (2012). Policy, planning, and management for religious tourism in Indian pilgrimage sites. *Journal of Policy Research in Tourism, Leisure and Events*, 4(3), 277-301. doi:10.1080/19407963.2012.726107
- Shinde, K. A., & Rizzello, K. (2014). A cross-cultural comparison of weekend-trips in religious tourism: insights from two cultures, two countries (India and Italy). *International Journal of Religious Tourism and Pilgrimage*, 2(2), 17-34.
- Smith, V. L. (1992). Introduction: The quest in guest. *Annals of Tourism Research*, 19(1), 1-17. doi:http://dx.doi.org/10.1016/0160-7383(92)90103-V
- Sørensen, A., & Babu, S. (2008). Tourism and the Informal Sector: Notes on the case of backpacker tourism. In S. Babu, S. Mishra, & B. B. Parida (Eds.), *Tourism Development Revisited: concepts, issues and paradigms* (pp. 88-102). New Delhi: Sage.
- Turner, V., & Turner, E. (1978). *Image and Pilgrimage in Christian Culture*. New York: Columbia University Press.
- Woodward, S. C. (2004). Faith and tourism: planning tourism in relation to places of worship. *Tourism and Hospitality Planning & Development*, 1(2), 173-186.

# IDENTIFYING PRIMARY AREAS OF GOVERNMENT MAL-FUNCTIONING IN NAXAL AFFECTED DISTRICTS OF ODISHA

Governance issues in the inaccessible and remote forested areas of the districts of Odisha have been a cause of concern for most administrators and concerned civilian activists. Numerous developmental programmes have been planned for the socio-economic upliftment of this population. However, often the reach of the programmes are not felt in the interior areas. Only after these programmes are effectively implemented can their effectiveness be aptly studied. If they don't reach the targeted population, the very essence is lost and so there is no point in assessing their efficiency or gauging the effectiveness of these developmental programs.

The benefits of the government programs often do not

reach these areas due to many factors reinforcing each other. Killing and kidnapping of government officials have demoralized the government functionaries to work in these areas. Except anti- extremist police task force, these areas are not visited much either by the forest officials, government officials, NGOs, or by outside civilians. As a result, these areas are extremely neglected. They have entered into a negative vicious circle of initial mal-governance leading to anti-government movement by the Maoists, leading in turn to Maoist threat to government officials resulting in further mal-governance. A major concern is that these forest dwellers are being allured by the Maoist groups into their fold by consistently criticizing the maladministration of the government agencies and gradually inducting them to their ideological fold.

Government has to adopt different strategies to handle the Maoist menace. It can either be offensive measures through use of force to annihilate the ultras ; the second approach is to usher in actual development into these areas. Since, in most of the Maoist hit areas the government functioning has come to a standstill, there is a need to identify the priority areas and strategize policies to regain the confidence of the targeted population.

This study was undertaken to ascertain the status of government programs and to determine the actual poverty level of these rural and forest dwellers in the interior Maoist hit areas of Odisha. Presently, only the police is able to reach these remote areas, where other government agencies have apprehensions in visiting due to the regular Naxal threats. During the regular patrolling and area dominance operations to flush out the Maoists, police could interact with the local population and collect information regarding their socio-economic status. Therefore, an attempt was made to analyse the response of residents of these interior areas on matters pertaining to their livelihood as well as pertinent governance issues.

**The Questionnaire:**

A questionnaire was developed to study the socio-economic status of poor people in the Naxal affected districts of Debgad, Dhenkanal, Koraput and Malkangiri districts of Odisha. The analysis was carried out to assess the human resource development index as well as the Governance Development Index.

The Human Resource Development Index includes the educational qualification, dwelling house, caste, economic conditions, and happiness quotient.

The Governance Development Index includes the utilization of government facilities by the local population and their rankings. The government departments included in the study are Schools, Hospitals, PDS, Blocks, Police, Forest, Veterinary, Agriculture, Anganwadi (Child Care), and Court.

The impressions of the respondents regarding the performance of different government agencies was collected. It is similar to citizens' perception index on government agencies. The questionnaire also tried to elicit their happiness quotient in life as per the five stage Likert scale. Household asset study was also included to know their economic status and living conditions. Questions related to family size, literacy, causes of poverty, money lending, labour migration, nutrition status, sanitation, etc, were also included in the questionnaire. The data was collected through interview technique to enable the respondents feel easy and confident.

The research sample

The geographical set up of the sample areas are

inaccessible and forested land. The study has included primitive tribes like, Kondhs, Kolhas, Mundas, Juangas, etc. The sample population was selected during field visits to Naxal affected areas. Mostly they have been identified from lower income groups belonging to ST's and SC's and are daily labourers, farmers, forest dwellers etc. They were randomly selected. Very few lady respondents could be included due to their shyness in giving interviews. Many tribal youth from the Naxal affected districts of Koraput and Malkangiri have been appointed as special police officers in the Police Training College at Angul. After surrendering, some of the ex-naxal cadre members are also taking training as Special Police Officers. They also comprised part of the sample. As a result this study includes the sample population from the Naxal affected districts of Dhenkanal, Deogarh, Koraput and Malkangiri. Koraput , Malkangiri and Deogarh are seriously affected by Naxal movement, where as Dhenkanal is partially affected by it.

**The study:**

The study was carried out to analyze the status of human resource indices in the Naxal affected areas. The status of government Service Delivery Indices was also found through the citizens' perception index. Later on these were mapped through cross tabulation with the help of SPSS software to identify the relationship between these indices.

The sample population is dominated by ST, SC and OBC (48%,20% and 26% respectively). The Human Development Index is shown in the charts below.

The Government Service Delivery Indices are as follows:

Analysis was carried out regarding availing government

facilities with respect to hospital, school, agriculture/ distribution system, block, electricity, banking facilities, anganbadi (child care), police, court, veterinary and forest departments. The ranking by the individual respondents was also analyzed to assess their perception about the functioning of different government departments.

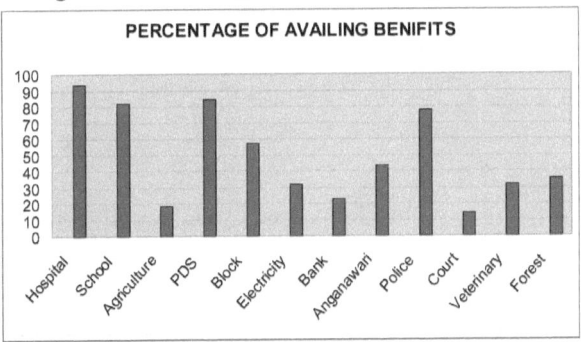

**HOSPITAL**

Only 9% have not availed hospital facility and out of the remaining 91%, 7% are not happy (2) and 7% not at all happy (1). However, 26%, 26%, and 22% are less happy(3), moderately happy(4) and very happy(5) respectively. The figure – shows the citizens's perception on Hospital Facilities. Those who have spent more in health sector (1- health, 2- Marriage, 3- health and marriage, 4- any other) have also given high rating to government hospitals (figure ).

Figure -

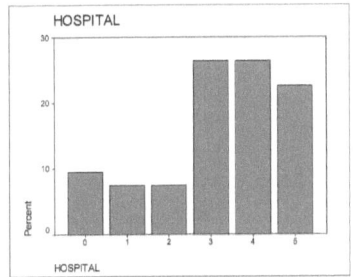

Figure - Cross tabulation high expenditure and hospital.

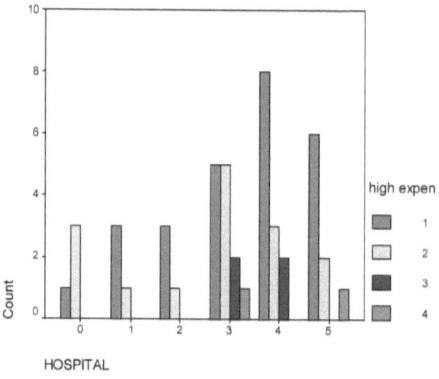

## SCHOOL

The frequency analysis for school facility shows that 22% have not availed these facilities. Out of the rest 78%, 4% each are not happy or not at all happy. However, 13%, 26% and 30% are less happy, moderately happy and very happy respectively (Figure - ). The caste and education cross tabulation showed that the SC community (2) are poor in education and none have gone beyond matriculation. STs (1) fare better to SCs in this respect. The OBC (3) and General castes (4) are better in education. This may be due to a greater degree of awareness among them. General Castes don't appear in illiterate (0) or under matriculate (1) category.

Figure -

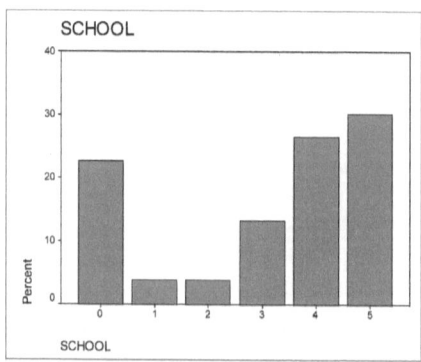

Figure –

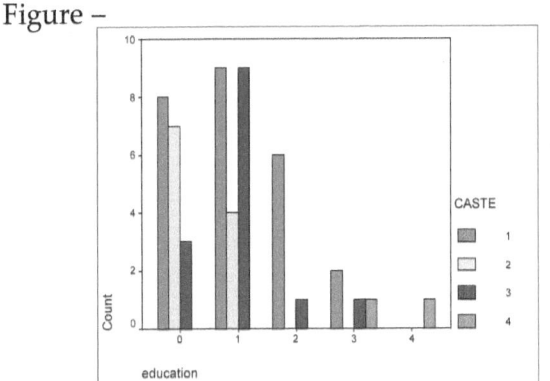

The cross tabulation between surplus and educational qualification reveals that if there is no surplus then studies do not progress beyond matriculation. This is shown in the figure - . It means that the drop out rate will decrease only when the family has a surplus to sustain the education of their children.

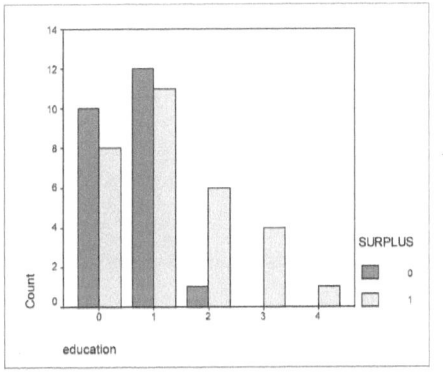

### AGRICULTURE

83% have not availed the facilities provided by the agriculture department and out of rest 17%, 8% are not happy and only 8% are happy. Figure - . Agriculture department has not been successful in penetrating into the interior areas.

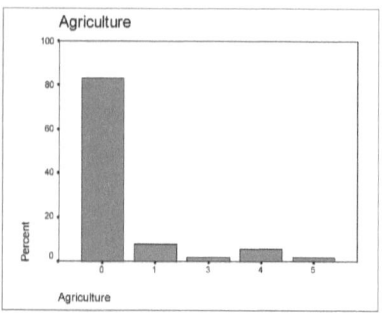

## PUBLIC DISTRIBUTION SYSTEM

16% of the respondents have not availed Public Distribution facility. Out of rest 84%, 40% are not happy or not at all happy. However, 16%, 20% and 30% are less happy, moderately happy and very happy respectively. The reason for happiness is that some are getting the kerosene and rice without card. The major reasons of unhappiness are untimely supply of PDS items and the fact that either they get rice and not kerosene or vice versa. The cross tabulation between the purchase pattern (1- daily, 2- twice a week, 3- weekly, 4- monthly) and PDS ranking showed that PDS ranking increased as the purchasing frequency increased from daily to weekly. The chart is shown in figure - .

Figure -

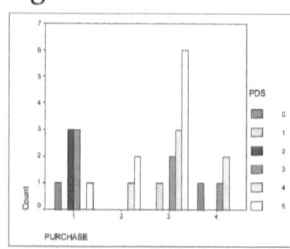

## BLOCK WORK

43% people are not aware of Block work and out of rest 57%, 23% people are not happy or not at all happy. Whereas, 9%, 14% and 11% are either happy, moderately happy and very happy.

## ELECTRICITY

A large segment of people, i.e. 68% have not availed electricity facility and remain in darkness and out of the rest 32%, 5% are either not happy or not at all happy where as 7%,13% and 7% are either happy moderately happy and very happy.

## BANK

A major chunk of the population,77% do not avail banking facility. Out of the rest 23%,4.5%and 9% are either less happy , moderately happy with the banking system. No one has expressed satisfaction regarding the banking facilities.

## ANGANBADI

As high as 57% of people do not avail Anganbadi facility in their village. Out of 43% ,5% are not happy or not at all happy whereas 4.5% , 18% and 16% are either happy, moderately happy with the Anganbadi facility.

## POLICE

23% people have not expressed their comments about the functioning of police in their area. Among the remaining respondents, 77% and 18% are not happy or not at all happy. 16%,29% and 14% are either happy , moderately happy or very happy with the police.

## COURT

As high as 84% have not availed the Court facility. Out of rest 16%, 2.5% are not happy with the Court functioning where as 4.5%,2% and 4.5% are either happy , moderately happy or very happy.

## VETERINARY

As high as 68% have not availed the Veterinary facility; out of rest 32%, 2% people are not happy with the Veterinary system where as 5%,9% and 16% are either happy , moderately happy or very happy.

## FOREST

64% people have no interaction with the forest department. Out of rest 36%, 7% people are not happy, not at all happy where as 20%, 7% are happy or very happy with the functioning of forest department.

Human Resource indices vis-à-vis Service Delivery indices

The study has been carried out through a cross tabulation of some indices of Service Delivery with human resources.

The sample population is dominated by ST's, SC's and OBC's (48%, 20% and 26% respectively). Around 30% are landless and 70% have agricultural land. 47% live in houses with thatched roofing, 15% asbestos, 22% tile roofing, where as 15% with RCC roofing. 58% population live in two room houses, 17% in 3 rooms and 8% in single room houses. Cross tabulation between roofing and agricultural land shows that those having agricultural land have better roofing like tile and RCC. The landless people having RCC are inhabiting Indira Awas houses. But they are too less and fail to cater to the requirements of the very poor sections of people in the interior areas. From the cross tabulation of RCC roofing and agricultural land, it is evident that only 12.5% of the landless people are awarded with the Indira Awas houses. This is in fact too low.

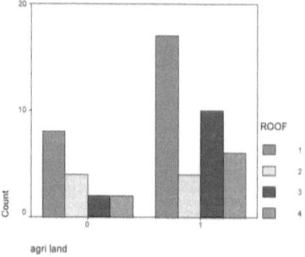

Similarly, the cross tabulation of factors like

Agricultural land and BPL indicates that 31% of the landless people are possessing BPL cards. The cross tabulation between agricultural land and NREGS shows that only 16% of the NREGS card holders are landless people. None of the landless people having NREGS cards have got work.

Another cross tabulation between two other factors- surplus and BPL card showed that majority of BPL card holders are those having surplus. People without surplus are deprived of the BPL cards as shown in figure - . Access to BPL card can reduce the expenditure on food and can generate surplus. This figure is substantiating that hypothesis. Like the success of the food stamp in USA, BPL card may be a good intervention to improve the quality of living by reducing expenditure on food.

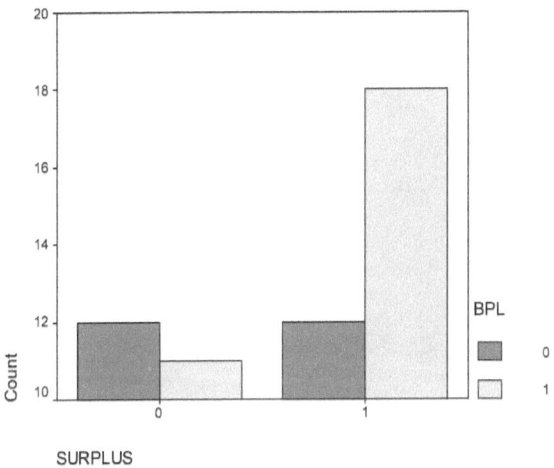

Similarly, it is observed that if there is no agricultural land, then there is no surplus. Only people having agricultural land have surplus. Some landless people also have surplus and they are either labourers, traders (fish sellers), skilled laborers (electrician), or women.

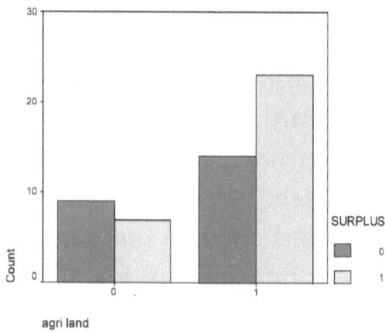

The cross tabulation between the purchase pattern (1- daily, 2- twice a week, 3- weekly, 4- monthly) and land holding showed that landless people go for daily purchasing and the land holders go for weekly purchasing (may be in the weekly markets). The chart is shown in figure - . This is also evident from the cross tabulation of surplus generation and the purchasing pattern as shown in figure - . As the surplus increases people switch from daily purchasing to weekly purchasing.

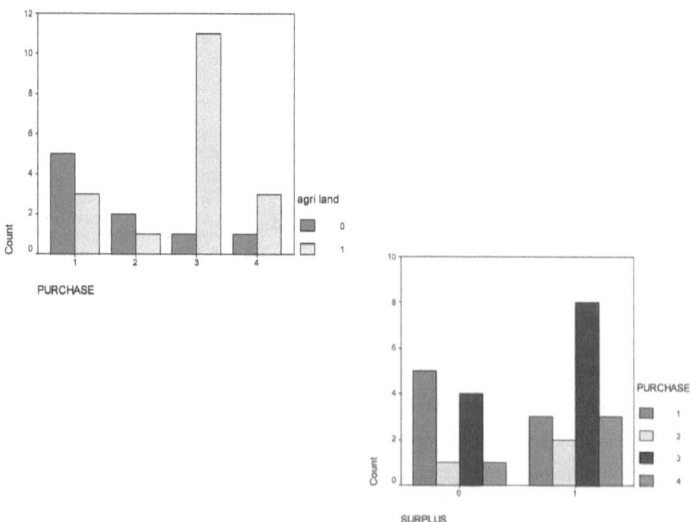

Further, the cross tabulation between purchase pattern and ranking of PDS showed that only those who go for weekly purchase give good rating to PDS as shown in the figure - . Those who purchase daily give low ranking as they are not in a position to accumulate enough money to buy PDS items.

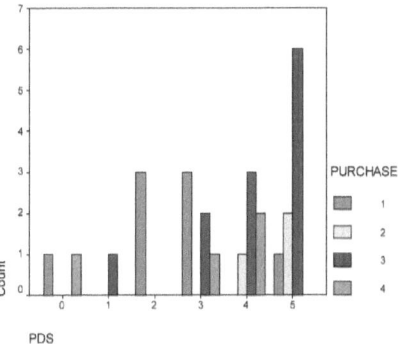

On another point, the cross tabulation between Land holding and PDS ranking showed that while the owners of land holdings give good ranking to PDS , the land-less give poor ranking as shown in the figure - . It can thus be interpreted that people possessing land are better beneficiaries of the PDS than the landless . It may be ascertained that landless people are poor users of the government delivery system.

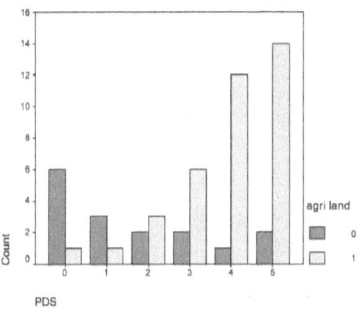

The landless people spend comparatively less on health

and marriage than people possessing land. Landless people don't avail other loans like agricultural, educational or for any allied activities, probably due to low net worth. Another important observation evident from the cross tabulation of landholding and liability is that landless people have less liability than people possessing land. The landless are in the grip of a vicious circle- no land holding causes low net worth and therefore, they are prevented from availing loans, consequently resulting in less liability. Same is the observation on the cross tabulation between surplus and liability as shown in figure - . Only people with surplus have liability.

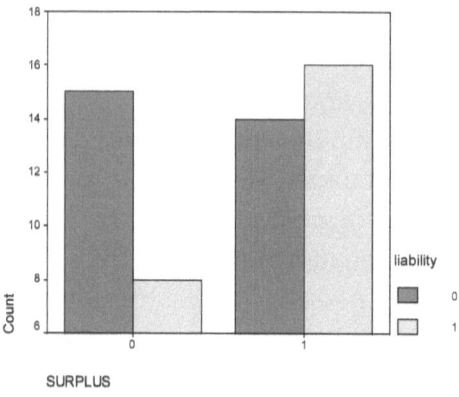

With regard to landholding the SC's are poorly placed. Only 55% among them are land holders and 45% , landless; however, among ST's and OBC's more than 70% own land.

Another tell-tale characteristic of the landless is that they are either illiterate or under-matriculate. None of the landless people in the chosen sample size was found to be a matriculate or above. Therefore, landholding and thereby financial stability has a significant role in influencing the pattern of education. This trend is also reflected with reference to the factors of caste and education. The SC's having negligible or no land are correspondingly poor in education. None of them have been educated beyond matriculation.

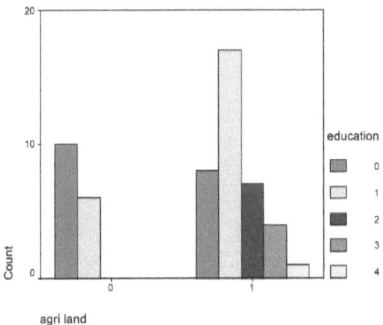

Further, the cross tabulation between number of rooms and agricultural land showed that landless people don't go beyond two rooms in their houses. Only land-owners can afford more rooms as shown in the figure - .

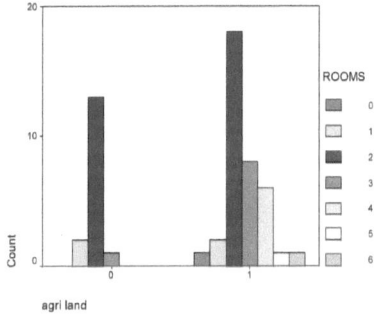

Economically 55% have no loan liability. The highest expenditure is in the health sector (55%), marriage (30%), both marriage and health 9%. The cross tabulation between liability and happiness showed that those having no liability are happier people. Among the unhappy, 50% are burdened by liability and 30% are free from it.

The cross tabulation between surplus and happiness showed that those having surplus are happier as indicated in the figure - .

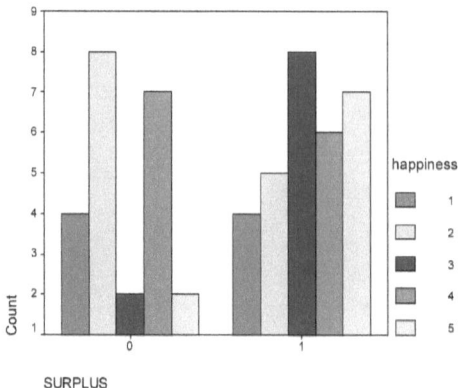

Respondents who have reaped surplus have experienced a considerable improvement in their lifestyle over the last three years, as shown in the figure - .People without surplus just maintain status-quo and don't find any noticeable improvement in their lifestyle.

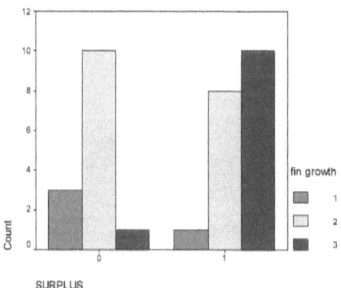

It was observed that those having road connectivity, either morrum or pucca are more likely to generate surplus as shown in the figure -. A potential contributing factor could be that the access to the outside world to sell the produce or the labour, increases manifold with the road connectivity.

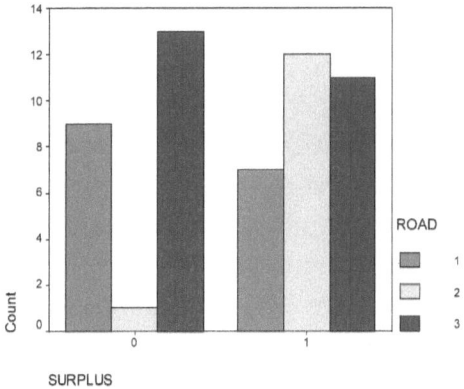

Cross tabulation between surplus and high expenditure showed that people without surplus have experienced high expenditure in health sector and low on marriage related expenditure. By comparision, those with surplus have incurred high expenses both in health as well as marriage as shown in the figure -.

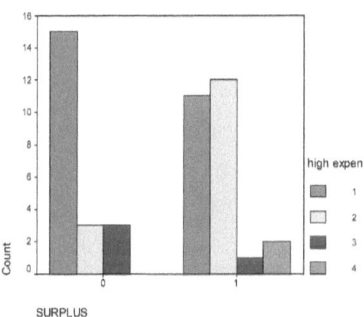

## Conclusion

From the analysis, it is definite that the Naxals focus more on settling land disputes and preventing construction of roads and thus connectivity into Naxal affected areas. They gain confidence of the local people by amicably settling their land dispute which could have taken years had they gone for civil cases in the modern government system. Naxals also hold Praja Courts to settle criminal cases, fine the accused persons and in the process deliver instance justice to the people which is most appealing to them.

As evident from the study, ownership of land has a greater impact on the life style of the population, and so the government should try to give land to the landless especially as agriculture is the mainstay in these areas. The land holding can increase the educational standard, surplus generation, better housing etc.

Surplus generation is important to improve the standard of living of a person. The surplus generation has positive impact on the availing the government facilities like PDS, Schooling etc. People with surpluses are also happier people. People with surpluses only experience betterment in the quality of life over the years. Therefore, the bottom line is to generate surplus amongst the poorer people. This can be done either by giving them arable land or by imparting training in vocational skills, which can improve their employability.

It was also observed that the landless people are the poor user of the government delivery system, which was derived from the cross tabulation of PDS and the land holdings..

Secondly they stop construction of road network in the naxal area on the protest of police using those road to hinder naxal grow but they do not stop the functioning of hospital public distribution system retail counter, school or Anganbadi (Child care) in the naxal affected areas because they also get benefit out of the hospital facility and public distribution system. But the study shows that access to better road increases the likelihood of generating surpluses, which in-turn improve the quality of life over a period of time. May be the hidden agenda of Maoist's is to keep the people poor and down trodden to follow their path. Any one who experiences the betterment in the quality of life may pursuit the economic growth route than the armed struggle root.

A combination of NREGS and distribution of BPL cards can work in tandem to create surplus amongst the poorer strata of the people in the naxal affected areas. In addition to that proving better health care facilities and improved road connectivity can bring a change in the quality of live within a span of five years. This developmental model can work better in a focused manner to check the growth of naxal growth in the interior pockets.

# BACKPACKING TRAVEL CULTURE: REFLECTIONS OF INDONESIA

*"Twenty years from now you will be more disappointed by the things you didn't do than by the ones you did do. So throw off the bowlines, sail away from the safe harbor. Catch the trade winds in your sails. Explore. Dream. Discover."* – Mark Twain

As tourism comes of age, a greater number of people are realizing that their leisure and pleasure lies in undefined forms of tourism. Niche tourism, through image creation, helps destinations to differentiate their tourism products, create a USP and compete in an increasingly competitive and cluttered tourism environment. The new age traveler is redefining conventional market segments and revolutionizing the world of tourism products. The psychology of travel has touched all need levels identified by Maslow's theory of "Need hierarchy".

As Pico Iyer states in an essay (2000):

"We travel, initially, to lose ourselves; and we travel, next, to find ourselves. We travel to open our hearts and eyes and learn more about the world than our newspapers will accommodate. We travel to bring what little we can, in our ignorance and knowledge, to those parts of the globe whose riches are differently dispersed. And we travel, in essence, to become young fools again — to slow time down and get taken in, and fall in love once more...."

There can thus be any number of travel motivations, from the most acceptable to the outright scandalous spurring people on to wander-lust.

1. A break from routine
2. Relaxation
3. Antidote to stress
4. Sun, sand and beach
5. Recuperation/Convalescence
6. Health/Fitness
7. Family bonding
8. Interpersonal relations
9. Ethnic base
10. Social networking
11. Achievement orientation
13. Status and prestige
14. Self-discovery
15. Cultural
16. Education
17. Professional/Business
18. Wanderlust
19. Interest in foreign areas
20. Nature

Niggel and Benson (2007) reveal that backpackers are motivated by discoveries of novelty, gaining broad knowledge about the world, escape from everyday work, social interaction, as well as having good times with friends. According to them the pull factors comprise native culture, adventure opportunities, climate, friendliness of the host population, beautiful beaches, available facilities and services, as well as the historical heritage of the host country.

Loker-Murphy and Pearce (1995: 830-831) offer one of the earliest academic definitions when they say, Backpackers are travellers who exhibit a preference for budget accommodation; an emphasis on meeting other people , an adaptable and flexible travel schedule, longer holidays, and an emphasis on unplanned recreational activities.

Typically backpacking tourists are regarded as those travellers who reflect a preference for budget accommodation and with a flexible travel itinerary. They prefer longer span of holidays. This interpretation has been rejected by many tourism researchers as it too easily dismisses differences in the backpacking travel mix (what about the flash-packers? And what about those boutique budget seekers? It's not all 'shoestring' anymore). Backpacking has burgeoned into a predominant lifestyle which fits in not only the budget traveller's desire "to get money's worth" but also the lifestyle statement of the rich. For those seeking independence, who wish to travel the road less frequented, who wish to create their own unchartered history, it is the backpacker culture that is most alluring.

Backpackers or economy travellers or young international independent travellers, are becoming very much noticeable in the tourism trade and scholarly materials (Pearce, 1990; Ateljevic & Doorne, 2004; Richards Wilson, 2005). Pearce (1990) states that backpacker travel is on the rise and has the potential of providing additional benefits complementary to other forms of tourism to the host destination. Over the past decade, backpackers have shifted out from the policy shadows and the confines of the travel and tourism trade into global interest (Richards & Wilson, 2005).

The typical backpacker tourist is well-educated and has a desire to travel as a "son of the soil", living and eating like the locals, not constrained by plans and itineraries, not to be trapped by packages and readymade experiences. Essentially regarded as a post-modern trend, it consists of highly mobile tourists in search of an identity.

## ESSENTIAL CHARACTERISTICS:
- use budget accommodation
- are involved in longer holidays
- are predominantly young
- have flexibility in their itineraries and
- show a willingness for group and social holiday activities.

## HISTORICAL EVOLUTION OF BACKPACKING TRAVEL:

Viewed as a 'rite of passage' for many, the transition of backpackers from 'drifter' to 'independent mass tourist', 'explorer' to 'sanitized' tourism alternative', also to 'budget travellers' and 'long-term travellers' has been traced through academic research. Backpacking has developed as a mainstream travel trend that has taken shape by adapting suitably to economic, social, technological and political trends both at home as well as the host societies.

The origin of the backpacker travelers can be traced as far back as the hunters and food gatherers. The tendency for wandering and exploring the unseen, unknown world has prevailed since long. The backpacker travel segment included predominantly young, budget tourists on extended holidays (Loker-Murphy & Pearce, 1995). Maoz and Bekerman (2010, p. 426) describe backpackers as 'relatively young tourists who tend to gather in ghettos or enclaves: places where large numbers congregate to experience home comforts and the company of tourists of similar interests.'

Hunters and food gatherers: Probably the earliest backpackers were the nomadic hunters and food gatherers. They had no itinerary or plan to bind them. They travelled with the wind and the seasons, across deserts and forests and found food on the way. Australian aborigines, South African Bushmen, Pygmy Tribes of the Congo, Native Americans, and certain other tribes across the world are all variants of the nomadic migrant. They found shelter in caves and rock formations, depending on the natural environment. The essential difference was that they travelled in search of survival rather than leisure or identity.

Explorers: Since the earliest times of civilization, adventurous explorers have wandered far and wide in search of novelty. There were no travel blogs or guides for these daring travellers who dared enter dense jungles, confront dangerous animals, malaria infested regions, snowy avalanches or desert storms for the pleasure of knowing the unknown.

The arrival of the backpacker: The Hippie trail which started around the sixties brought forth the questioning traveller who set out for spiritual enlightenment, in search of God, identity or even solitude. The routes spanned from the cobbled stone ways of nondescript European villages to Asia's rich historical heritage, from the Silk route to Indian bazaars to Nepal's Buddhist monasteries. Travellers lived with the locals, ate their food and got to know their way of life.

Modern backpacking: The backpacker travel segment

has burgeoned beyond imagination in recent times. With growing stress, nuclear and broken families, travel decisions are taken independently. Backpacking today is a style statement. The interpretation of one's identity and how we relate to destinations has undergone radical transformation Travel is the dream-boat for the spiritual traveler or the healer.

## BACKPACKING TRAVEL CULTURE:

E.B. Taylor defined culture as "that complex whole which includes knowledge, belief, art, morals, laws, customs, and many other capabilities and habits acquired by...[members] of society."

Cultural patterns and values of destinations influence visitor behavior in varied ways. In the global pot-pourri of culture, traditional cultural patterns do not necessarily perish but are recreated by a fusion with other cultures. From the nomadic hunters and food gatherers to the Greeks and Romans travelling for leisure, from a pass-time of the elite to mass tourism, several travel patterns have evolved. Back-packing is a post-modern travel trend rapidly gaining popularity not just as a travel pattern but a life-style and a form of mainstream travel.

The backpacker society is characterized by certain essential cultural components, as reflected by the field work conducted by Anders Sorensen like hierarchy, specific symbols of exchange, certain unique practices, exchange of travel information and a specific backpacker ideology. Anderskov(2002) found a hierarchically structured backpacker culture where individual status was connected to indicators like tolerance, interaction with the host population and access to travel information. International travellers who are backpacking are normally found to be at critical junctures of life like loss of job, pre-marriage, post-divorce, loss of family member etc. However they always indicate the desire to return to normal life.

The backpacker's culture must necessarily "travel" (Clifford 1997). The concept of road culture is used to identify the backpacker(Adler 1985; Mukerji 1978; Riley 1988)."Authenticity" is a key variable in the cultural setting of a back-packer. Authenticity refers to the extent to which one is honest to one's own personality, spirit, or character, despite external constraints. The desire to be a participant in the local culture, be it the boat-men(Nolia's) of Puri to the perishing tuk-tuk's of Cambodia to the struggling artisan's shops of Borobudur is a hallmark of this form of travel.

"Tourism is so much about the production of dreams, the indulgence in fantasies and escapism into ideal worlds" (Smith, 2003: 175). Interestingly, backpackers choose to escape to the Third World where conditions of poverty and hardship are idealized by the backpacker to constitute a reality, or authenticity, which is not available to them in the modern, developed world they come from. France's post-modern theorist Jean Baudrillard considers backpacking tourism, which has been criticized as a form of poverty tourism (Scheyvens, 2001:150), to represent an attempt at 'catastrophe management' by the 'rich' of the West (Baudrillard, 1994:66). He explains, "We (in the west) are the consumers of the ever delightful spectacle of poverty and catastrophe, and of the moving spectacle of our own efforts to alleviate it" (Baudrillard, 1994:67).

### BACKPACKING VALUES:

Values are commonly held notions in a culture about what is acceptable and unacceptable code of conduct. They are "prescriptive" and "proscriptive" beliefs of "ethical" goals which cultures strive for. They are the fundamental basis for beliefs and are an extremely important factor in uniting cultures (Macionis and Plummer 2008, p.125). Values are an enduring, essential element of culture that are slow to change (Penguin Dictionary of Sociology 2006, p.409). They are learned by the members of a society through a process called socialization, which occurs in various institutions in society such as family, schools and religious organizations. How we interpret events and interactions is dictated by our values; furthermore they greatly influence our moral views. They play a large part in defining how we act in our various roles in society (Macionis and Plummer 2008, p.125).

Freedom, independence, low budget, tolerance and interaction with locals, are the five basic values of the backpackers. Most other values seemed to arise from these five basic values, and combined they form a whole set of values. Backpacker values and beliefs are all linked to a new interpretation of "status" on road. Paying "local prices", effective "haggling", extended travel, getting off the beaten track, tales of exotic illnesses and unusual experiences are only some of the ways in which it is possible to gain road status (Sorensen 2003p.856)

The new backpacker: the post-modern individual is a global nomad and his efforts to deal with inevitable change is the new backpacker's story.

## BACKPACKING AND CONSTRUCTION OF TOURIST IDENTITY:

The new–age traveller is the one who questions everything he comes across and is swamped by self-doubt. Not for him the predictability of conventional travel patterns or living styles. In an attempt to redefine the self with backpacking, the backpacker has become a popular cultural symbol of the recent times.

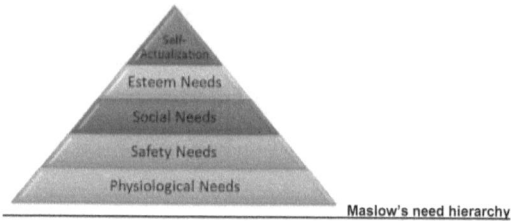

Maslow's need hierarchy

The backpacker could travel for any or all of the need categories outlined by Maslow. The backpacker's travel motivation is a blend of all these need categories, though they could also be focused on anyone of them. The backpacker's travel motivations could span an entire gamut of needs: a desire to get away from the grind of life, a desire to know and see more, one's inner yearning for solitude and space.

Pearce applied Maslow's model of needs to tourism and combined it with the tourist's experience. He identified five layers of holiday motivations (from the bottom to the top of the pyramid):

Rejuvenation, exploration and relaxation are oft-quoted motives stimulating travel in this segment. The new age traveller(the backpacker) is the one who is willing to negotiate identities. There is the need to redefine one's image. Meaningful identity constructions give meaning to the traveller's life. It is through symbolic consumption patterns through tourism that the traveller moulds his identity. As indicated by Ostergaard and Jantzen in consuming tourism products and services, the traveller uses the fabric of emotions and feelings to create a coherent life. For the spiritual backpacker, travel experiences help in shaping the "self".

*What happens when disenchanted or alienated individuals become growingly aware of their state of alienation, and the meaninglessness and fatuity of their daily life, as many younger members of the middle classes in "postmodern" society have become? One direction in their search for meaning might take is the attempt to transform their society through revolution; another, less radical alternative is to look for meaning in the life of others – tourism. The renewed quest for meaning, outside the confines of one?s own society, is commenced* (Cohen, 1979, p.11).

Often the consequence is an unintentional transformation of the self. There is also a state of inner bliss and self-actualization one attains in the process of self-identity creation.

"Self-Fulfillment" is a state where travellers set out to achieve a personal goal/challenge and reflect upon accomplishment. "A musician must make music, an artist must paint, a poet must write, if he is to be ultimately happy. What a man can be, what he must be. This need we may call self-actualization" (Maslow, 1943, p. 383).

## REFLECTIONS OF INDONESIA: YOGYAKARTA/ BOROBUDUR

Backpacker culture is one defined as "Going with the wind".A backpacker tourist writes his own piece of culture and tries to create it, strategically utilizing the backdrop of the destination and its culture to weave experiences that enrich life.Ever since the counter-cultural movement of the sixties, Southeast Asia has steadily drawn backpackers to its fold, what with its unique tapestry of ancient civilizations as well as the unimaginably low prices for western travelers.

The author's account of her experience with backpackers at Indonesia:

I did not travel to Yogyakarta (popularly referred to as Jogja) as a backpacker but as a cultural tourist, to unravel it's miraculous inheritance of Borobudur and Prambanan temples.While there, I got to mingle with a group of backpackers from different parts of Europe and US. Most of them were in their thirties, avid travellers and in search of spiritual enlightenment. We decided to be together for our visits to Prambanan and Borobudur.

Atop Borobudur(UNESCO world heritage site): Magelang, Central Java, Indonesia

Unique aspects of backpacking observed:

The experience is of utmost importance: I found the group sharing personal experiences connected with the need to self-actualize by the travel to Borobudur.The historical heritage became the perfect backdrop for accentuating the need for creating an identity. many philosophical questions were discussed on the topmost platform of Borobudur, with the life-size Buddha statues as the only witness.

To see the most within the constraints of budget.: The spirit of the group was indefatigable. They wanted to see every bit of the temple complex of Prambanan nad Borobudur. From the rare sight of sunrise atop the hill Bukit Punthuk Setumbu, to exploring every plaque in every level of Borobudur, the steep climb up all temples of Prambanan to watching the Ramayan theatre group, everything was part of the "must do" list.

Assimilation with the local culture, cuisine and people: Being in the heartland of Javanese culture left us with no option but to try out everything that the local culture offered- watching the classical music and dance show at the The Kraton Ngayogyokarto Hadiningrat (the Sultan's Palace), exploring the batik bazaar, traditional crafts, and trying out the traditional dishes( Gudeg,Gado Gado, Kupat Sayur, the list is endless) at wayside restaurants.

Entertainment and thrill: I found the group of backpackers very open to new adventure, from unknown hiking trails to scaling Mt.Merapi.

Enhanced social skills: Not only did the group communicate with each other but easily mingled with the locals as well. It brings to an end the prejudice that cultural stereotypes can at times create. Forging new friendships, facing crisis, dealing with stress and cross-cultural issues all make the backpacker a well-rounded personality with a meaning ful social network.

Construction/Reconstruction of self-identity and through that, self-actualization.

Quoting Jerry(backpacker from Cologne,Germany)

*"Jogja gave me a sense of adventure, something I hadn?t done before. Ever since I read about the way Borobudur was affected by the Merapi volcanic eruption,I wanted to walk the same trail.It gave me a sense of thrill, an excitement, a feeling I could'nt have had at home".*

- Bauman, Zygmunt. 1997: "Postmodernity and its Discontents", New York, New York University Press.
- Bauman, Zygmunt. 1996: "From Pilgrim to Tourist - or a short History of Identity", in Hall, Stuart and Paul du Gay: "Questions of Cultural Identity", London, Sage Publications.
- Bruner, Edward M. 1995: "The Ethnographer/Tourist in Indonesia", in Lanfant, Marie Farncoise,
- Allock, John B. and Edward, Bruner M. (Eds.): "International Tourism: Identity and Change", London, Sage Publications Ltd.
- Cohen, Erik. 1973: "Nomads from Affluence: Notes on the Phenomenon of Drifter-Tourism", International Journal of Comparative Sociology, vol. 14, no. 1, p. 89-103.
- Cohen, Erik (2003). "Backpacking: Diversity and Change"(PDF). *Tourism and Cultural Change* **1** (2): 95–110. Retrieved2007-10-29.
- Deforges, Luke. 2000: "Travelling the World: Identity and Travel Biography", Annals Of Tourism Research, vol. 27, no. 4, p. 926-945.
- Friedman, Jonathan. 1994: "Cultural Identity and

Global Process", London, Sage Publications.
- Lash, Scott and John Urry. 1999: "Economies of Signs and Space", London, Sage Publications Ltd.
- Loker-Murphy, L. and Philip L. Pearce. 1995: "Young Budget Travellers: Backpackers in Australia", Annals of Tourism Research, vol.22, no. 4, p. 819-843.
- McGregor, Andrew. 2000: "Dynamic Texts and Tourist Gaze: Death, Bones and Buffalo", Annals of Tourism Research, vol. 27, no. 1, p. 27-50.
- Miller, Robert L. 2000: "Researching Life Stories and Family Histories", London, Sage Publications.
- Murphy, Laurie. 2001: "Exploring Social Interactions of Backpackers", Annals of Tourism Research, vol. 28, no. 1, p. 50-67.
- Riley, Pamela J. 1988: "Road Culture of International Long-Term Budget Travelers", Annals of Tourism Research, vol.15, no.3, p.313-328.
- Siebers, Hans. 2000: "Thinking Together What Falls Apart: Some Reflections on the Concept of Identity", in Driessen, Henk and Ton Otto (eds.): "Perplexities of Identification", Århus, Århus University Press.
- Sørensen, Anders. 1999: "Travellers in the periphery: Backpackers and other independent multiple destination tourists in peripheral areas", Bornholm, Bornholms Forskningscenter.
- Sørensen, Anders. 1992a: "Travellers i Sydøstafrika - en etnografisk introduktion", fieldwork thesis, Århus University, Moesgaard, Department of Ethnography and Social Anthropology.
- Urry, John. 1995: "Consuming Places", London, Routledge.

# CIVIC GOVERNANCE: AESTHETICS AND AMENITIES- DESTINATION ODISHA

- Is civic tourism another exercise in complaining about how tourism "changed our cities" ? No- that approach only builds walls we are trying to tear down.
- It is fostering a constructive dialogue about how we can inspire pride in an industry that has tremendous potential to enhance our communities historic and environmental assets; at the same time inspiring in the industry a corresponding pride in the place in which it woks.
- It would be ideal to think of tourism as an ecosystem, where the ingredients of place contribute to our long-term economic viability. Damage one cog in the wheel and the entire machine grinds to a halt.
- Some of our best tourist experiences are not derived from the quality of the "tourism attraction", but where residents are welcoming, because they are proud of their "home" and wish to share it.
- So, this is a two-way street: citizens care about a business

that markets their home; at the same time, the industry learns about the values and stories that define the environment in which it works.

The concept of civic tourism begins with what some might consider an impossible claim, that tourism, one of the largest industries in the world, could help communities preserve their quality of life. This is a suggestion that tourism could help protect neighbourhoods, save the environment, preserve cultures, and be an antidote to the much publicized retreat of the public from civic matters.

However, for a long time the process to create win-win partnerships between tourism and place-based groups (people and organizations that preserve the cultural, natural and built environments) had its contradictions.

Tourism is often caught in the "economic development" trap or "what we add". Whenever the industry gets defensive, or needs to marshal arguments, it invariably falls back on what tourism adds : money it brings, jobs it creates etc.

A survey conducted in Puri, Odisha suggests most residents would gladly trade tourism's economic benefits (and assets, like better restaurants) if they could have their old town back. Most hotels in Puri are out of place as they are not appropriate to the ingredients of the place, its history, natural setting and other built structures.

The market alone, absent a community based consideration of place should not be the sole voice of tourism development.

## 1. Differentiate

Differentiation *is* important. Towns in the tourism business are in "sales," trying to sell their town to potential customers (tourists). Most business consultants who advise companies on how to sell a product say they must "differentiate" in order to compete.

The irony is that while tourism towns are in sales, and therefore should distinguish their community from others, most places are beginning to look more and more alike. Civic tourism helps communities identify, develop, and use their distinguishing market niche.

## 2. Define "Place" Comprehensively

Heritage is only one part of "placed-based tourism," a phrase that includes other forms of tourism that see the region itself (its natural, built, and historic qualities) - not just "tourism attractions" - as the "product."

In addition to heritage, other approaches that fall under the "place-based" umbrella include the natural environment (ecotourism) and historic preservation (urbanism). Heritage tourism, ecotourism, and urbanism are important ingredients of a place-based tourism economy, but rarely do we find these groups working together, even though they all have preservation of place as a primary goal. Consequently, each of them relates to the tourism industry in a piece-by-piece or project-oriented way.

Civic Tourism shows these place-based sectors how to work together to create a form of tourism that is not "project" centered, but which privileges "place" as the main attraction. In effect, Civic Tourism creates a more focused way for these groups to interact with the tourism community - together, not as individual strands.

## 3. Invest in Product Development

Most tourism programs concentrate the majority of

their planning and funding on marketing. They invest countless hours and dollars in determining, designing, and distributing the best promotional strategies. Tax payers often subsidize this work, by underwriting local or statewide tourism agencies.

These tourism organizations generally say they don't do product development – they market. Fine, but if these agencies (those in charge of managing tourism for their community) don't provide direction or funding for product development, who does?

Civic Tourism maintains that we need to "close the circle" around tourism development. That is, just as the tourism industry invests in marketing, communities should invest equally in the product. That investment needs to be both conceptual (what is the product?) and financial (how do we build or enhance the product?).

## 4. Involve the Public

Advocates of Civic Tourism understand that many of their goals will not be realized unless there is a strong element of the public's voice underpinning this work. Place-based tourism demands community involvement because the story of "place" is, first of all, the story of people who live there.

Tourism campaigns are often established by a small group – chambers of commerce, tourism officials, city councils, hotels and restaurants. These players certainly have a say in the direction of their tourism program, but so should the general public – the people whose story defines the product, the people who are often most affected by tourism, who often know the most about their town's history, who are usually the most concerned about and committed to their community's future.

## Place as Product

Place is not just heritage, land or buildings – its all three together. It is important to overcome sectoral fragmentation because that keeps place-based groups separate and relatively toothless, and we miss the forest for the trees.

This is where Puri can excel, whether it's the majestic natural landscape of the seashore or the equally majestic cultural landscape of Konark.

*The tourism industry refers to "destinations". "Place" is more preferable and there's a cavernous difference between those words. As Jim Quay once said, place is a destination with a story. Destination implies: come, spend, leave – it's a dot on the map, and it perpetuates the drive by tourism that plagues too many of our towns. Place, though says: come, learn, get attached, spend, stay longer, leave – and return. It's easy to see this almost spiritual attachment at, say, Lord Jagannaths abode, our place is not a dot on the map; instead, it's an experience.*

Its unique experiences, not assembly-line settings that will create this emotional connection. And uniqueness is a by-product of the cultural, natural and historic assets particular to a place.

## Extending the Reach : The Civic Governance Process

The product is "civic" in that it's an agreed-upon sense of place; the process is also "civic", because it depends on a community conversation about what place is.

The discussion about how towns "do" tourism used to be a narrow one: the government, the industry or tourism department. When niches like heritage or ecotourism appeared, the conversation often broadened to include place-based voices, because tourism stakeholders rightly recognized that these are the "content" people, and engaging them gave tourism a better product to market.

The group still missing, though, is the public, the people who live in the places we market. Including residents in the discussion is a natural evolution.

If we're to inculcate civic pride in tourism, we have to educate the public about the industry, which surveys suggest people know little about; or else what they think they know is wrong. But that means doing more than talking at citizens; it means giving those who are often the most affected by the tourism industry's decisions a voice in how their town is bundled as an attraction.

Few things- from planning democracies to city streets – benefit by shutting citizens out. Thomas Jefferson had said: "I know of no safe depository of the ultimate powers of society but the people themselves; and if we think them not enlightened enough to exercise their control with a wholesome discretion, the remedy is not to take it away from them, but to inform their discretion by education".

There are lot of tourists coming to Odisha for the "Puri Experience", which includes the struggle of getting from place to place and the general chaos one encounters. If we want money tourists then we need to cater to their needs. These are families and elderly tour groups who come and expect clear-cut outcomes. Overall cleanliness, manageable delays (if any), a high degree of convenience, predictability and controllable situations (from the tourist point of view) and a net positive experience in terms of their expectations.

Are some of the glossy tourism promotion campaigns masking some ugly realities ? Most tourists returning from Odisha destinations report that they have been misled. Often the complaint is about dirty tourist amenities, far removed from what is usually depicted in official brochures. They also recall being hounded by beggars, fleeced by uncouth taxi drivesr and aggressive Puri Pandas. This fact has further been driven home by Subhash Goyal very recently, "Apart from sanitation, the state administration must ensure that pilgrims are not made to suffer by few unscrupulous elements in the Jagannath Temple premise. In the process, repeat visitors can easily be put off". A news item in Indian Express dated January 13$^{th\ 2005}$ reports a French tourist pointing out that polythenes and other synthetic material pollute the beach. Even more harrowing is the experience of tourists waking early to admire the beauty of sunrise along the seashore, only to witness the locals using the beach as an open toilet.

It would not be out of place to quote Shri Jagmohan, Ex-Minister for Tourism & Culture, who after his visit to Odisha in 2002, had commented : "Though endowed with natural beauty...... this long beach is in a state of neglect. Insanitary conditions prevail while odd structures have come up here and there; there is no proper shelter or public convenience for the tourists".

Regarding Chandrabhaga Beach, he had further stated : "A number of shacks and ugly stalls have come up near the sea line".

The stench emanating from hotel effluents, human and animal feces and animal carcasses welcomes a tourist.

Why do people travel ? They travel to fulfill their dreams and to look for serenity. It is okay to mix dreams with reality sometimes. But they should not be disproportionate.

Tourism should help eliminate poverty, unemployment and create new skills by synthesizing the elements of tourism, culture and clean civic life and focusing on constructive, focused and result oriented governance.

Another important area of focus is law and order. The

entire tourism industry has a vested interest in the safety of domestic and inbound international travelers. It is an investment in security that will help confirm the states reputation as a safe travel destination in the eyes of world travelers.

Bad roads, tackling traffic flow, vehicular pollution and the attendant health hazards need to be tackled with the same level of expertise and inter-disciplinary cooperation as any other public health problem.

Laws need to be enforced to ensure public cleanliness, otherwise tourists may never arrive. Moreover, India needs public cleanliness for its own citizens, not just for tourists.

Specifically the focus should be on :

- Infrastructure which facilitates clean, rapid and trouble free access to attractions.

- Special zones and tourist corridors to be created in and around attractions.

- Aesthetics and lung spaces : Parks should be developed to lend aesthetic appeal.

Attractive and user friendly bus shelters, polished granite benches, walkways, sanitary facilities.

The status of existing Urban Infrastructure in Odisha is as follows:

- City roads are inadequate leading to traffic congestion and poor ride quality. As against requirement of about Rs.30,000 crore per annum on infrastructure availability of resources is low.
- Areas of PPP are conservancy, sanitation, garbage collection and disposal, solid waste management, composting, street lighting, water supply, collection of local taxes, maintenance of gardens and parks, land development, promotion of market complexes, bus terminus etc.

- Lack of interest for e-governance relating to property taxes, accounting system, collection of water service charges, issue of birth and death certificates, sanction of building plans, management system for works programmes etc.
- Lack of community involvement for management of civic services and implementation of local projects, collection of taxes, fees and user charges as well as deployment of resources.

**New strategy for Urban Development**
- Convergence of all infrastructure assistance programmes
- Launching of national urban renewal mission
- Passage of community participation law to ensure active participation of the citizenry in area sabhas
- Introduction of e-governance including geographical information system and management information system
- Reform of property taxes
- Grant assistance would be leveraged to attract additional resources from the capital market
- Ensure efficiency of drinking water supply on the basis of water audit

**Reform measures:**

- Revision of bye-laws to streamline approval process for construction of building, development of sites
- Simplification of procedure for conversion of agricultural land to non-agricultural purpose
- Introduction of property title certification system
- Introduction of computerised registration of land and property

- Rain water harvesting to be made mandatory in all building plans
- Reuse of reclaimed water
- Adoption of water conservation measures
- Reduction in establishment costs and implementation of other administrative reforms measures
- Earmarking 25% of developed land for economically weaker sections
- Integrated Slum Development
- Projectization approach to be adopted for rehabilitation of slum colonies either in situ or else where
- Sustainability of slum development to be ensured through contribution of beneficiaries and involvement of financial institutions

**Recommendations for effective Civic Management**
- The state government along with major stake holders and NGOs may initiate constructive and proactive steps to strengthen civic governance in the state in general and at Bhubaneswar, Puri and Konark on a top-most priority basis.
- The urban renewal plans for the old cities in the state like Cuttack should be initiated with tourism as one of the central pillars that will serve the dual purposes of urban renewal and tourism product differentiation.
- The encroachment in all forms around the monuments, approach roads and other public places should be removed and the loss should be strictly implemented.
- High-priority should be given for evolving systems for sustainable management of the places through proper coordination between local bodies, government agencies and non-government organizations.

- The following recommendations are suggested to tackle the problem areas :
- Healthy and safe environment is essential for fostering the growth of travel and tourism.
- Travel and tourism companies should state their commitment to environmentally compatible growth.
- Identity and minimize product and operational environmental problems, paying particular attention to new projects.
- Pay due regard to environmental concerns in design, planning, construction and implementation.
- Be sensitive to conservation of environmentally protected or threatened areas, species and scenic aesthetics, achieving landscape enhancement where possible.
- Practice energy conservation
- Reduce and recycle waste
- Practice fresh-water management and control sewage disposal;
- Control and diminish air emissions and pollutants;
- Monitor, control and reduce noise levels,
- Control, reduce and eliminate environmentally unfriendly products, such as asbestos, CFC's, pesticides and toxic, corrosive, infectious, explosive or flammable materials;
- Respect and support historic or religious objects and site;
- Exercise due regard for the interests of local populations, including their history, traditions and culture and future development
- Consider environmental issues as a key factor in the overall development of Travel and Tourism destinations.

- To Opt for an honest and responsible marketing of tourism
- Provide better and more comprehensive training for tourist trade personnel
- Inform host population about tourists and the problems involved in tourism
· To prepare and educate people for travel.

We're in the product business; this is not about marketing better, but about re-articulating the thing we market; and most importantly, about creating the public and political will to advocate for and help us think about appropriate product development. Other than that, we have no grand scheme, no template that fits every community.

**Reference :**
- Wood E. Robert and Picard Michael (eds) Tourism, Ethnicity, and the state in Asian and Pacific Societies, 1997.
- Mowforth, Martin and Ian Munt. Tourism and Sustainability: New Tourism in the Third World, London: Routledge, 1998.
- MacCannel, Dean: The Tourist : A New Theory of the Leisure Class, 3rd Ed. Barkley: University of California Press, 1999
- Bosselman, Fred P., Craig A. Peterson, and Claric McCarthy. Managing Tourism Growth: Issues and Applications. Washington D.C. Island Press, 1999

# THE IMPACT OF ETHICAL POLICING

**ETHICS DEFINED**

From the perspective of Western tradition, the development of ethical theory dates back to Plato (427-347 B.C.) and Aristotle (384-322 B.C). The word *ethics* has its roots in the Greek work *ethos*, which means "customs", "conduct," or "character." Ethics is concerned with the kinds of values and morals an individual or society finds desirable or appropriate.

**PRINCIPLES OF ETHICAL LEADERSHIP**

There are five principles of ethical leadership, the origins of which can be traced back to Aristotle. Although not inclusive, these principles provide a foundation for the development of sound ethical leadership: *respect, service, justice, honesty* and *community.*

Leadership is the process of influencing others to reach a common goal. This requires that the leader and followers agree on the direction to be taken by the group. Leaders need to take into account their own and followers' purposes, while working toward goals that are suitable for both of them. This factor, "concern for others", is the distinctive feature that delineates *authentic* transformational leaders from pseudo-transformational leaders.Concern for the common good means that leaders cannot impose their will on others. They need to search for goals that are compatible with everyone.

A policeman cannot easily cast aside what he is taught from the very first day he joins the training institution as a probationer. He is, for example, taught that he is the proud upholder of the citizen's most jealously guarded possessions-his liberty and property. Repeatedly droned in his ears is his role of an objective and impartial keeper of public peace and investigation of the violations of law by the citizens without bias or prejudice, irrespective of the relative social, political or financial status of the parties involved. However, once he enters upon his duties in the field, he discovers how remote the ground realities are from all that he had been taught to believe. He discovers, too, that almost every institution created by the Constitution or the law has been subjected to remorseless manipulation by ambitious and unscrupulous politicians. The Constitution and its institutions are relevant to them only to the extent these can be utilized to ward off any possible threat to the privileges of those who are in power positions. The new entrant to the police sometimes discovers that equality before the law is a mere slogan. In reality, there are always some who must be understood to be more equal than the vast majority. Rules are exceptions and exceptions are the rules.

However, the experience of many ethically sound police officers has shown that the police can perform their duties strictly in accordance with law and can also control crime and maintain law and order. In India, the police image and reputation is at an all time low due to the unethical means used by policemen in solving pressing problems they face in day to day police work. A policeman must understand that he is basically a manager of social change. The Indian society is undergoing a metamorphosis and consequently, there are several social tensions prevailing. It requires a policeman of perspective and understanding to deal with such situations. Straightforward and honest policing has its own intrinsic strength. In case of a police dilemma, a deliberation on the various alternatives and course of action is possible in the framework of what can be called an Ethics Check. The Ethical Check consists of four questions:Is it legal? Is it just? Is it in public interest? How will it make me feel about myself?

Ethical policing has tremendous impact on everything having something to do with policing. When the police starts functioning with ethically sound principles many of the ills prevalent in the police organization vanish without any expense. The cutting edge level for the common man in the police organization is the police station. If any crime is committed or if any individual is harassed and aggrieved he approaches the police station. The minimum he expects from the police is that he is given a patient hearing and his case is registered. An ethically sound policeman will do it promptly and will be sensitive to his grievances.

Ethical behaviour by the policemen not only make them authentic and self-confident, but all pressures, administrative or political, also vanish. It can be said that the pressures are generated by the unethical behavior of policemen. If there is pressure from the top to control crime the Inspector has a temptation to minimize or conceal heinous offences like theft or robbery. If the source of pressure is removed the police work becomes smooth. The aggrieved start getting relief from policemen. The police station becomes functional. The public confidence in the police improves. Now the people start coming to the policemen directly for grievance redressal.

Ethical policing demoralizes the criminals. Criminals thrive on the protection they get from the politicians or the influential persons. But for the ethically sound policemen this protection becomes meaningless. When the policemen take action against criminals on the basis of facts and not on the basis of their connections the criminals become extremely weak, vulnerable and shelter-less. When action is taken against the known and protected criminals, other criminals stop committing crime on their own.

The best beneficiary of ethical policing will be the common man. The policemen will listen to them as their masters and their well being and welfare will become a policeman's first priority. They will become the people's police.

Like the problems that affect the moral fabric of our society, there are no quick fixes to the problem of police integrity. The issue is far too complex for easy answers. However, the police community can take concrete steps that can have a significant effect upon the problem.

### *Organizational Climate Supportive of Ethical Behaviour*

Formulating a code of conduct is an essential first step in establishing an ethical work environment. Beyond this, the police department must establish a climate within the organization in which integrity is not only possible, but is actually nurtured and rewarded. There are several aspects to this.

**To Foster Consistency:** Police departments must be careful to guide their officials in a manner that is at all times consistent with values, policies and procedures that have been developed. The department must make certain that officers adhering to the proper standards are rewarded, and that officers failing to adhere to those standards are censured. Any failure to observe this basic principle indicates to departmental personnel that the department's values are selectively applicable, and violations of the code of conduct may not be reasonably enforced or may even be ignored under certain situations.

**Recruiting:** It should be noted that it is vital that the recruiting process do more than just bring in persons who score well on psychological tests, pass a medical examination, and lack a criminal record. The use of psychological and personality profiles have become a standard recruiting tool, but, unfortunately, these tests are more useful for screening out those who are clearly unqualified than in identifying those who are the best qualified for police work.

The recruiting process should stress the importance of hiring (and retaining) not just those who survive screening tests and background checks, but also those who have demonstrated in the past their interest and involvement in activities that reveal a concern for the community and its people. The world of policing is changing, and the coming years are, inevitably, going to bring a demand from our society for a police force that is more sensitive to the needs of the community and those who live in it. Therefore, when recruiting new officers in the years to come, a willingness to serve the community in ways that go beyond traditional conceptions of criminal apprehension will be an essential trait of a good police officer. A background that reveals a recruit's motivation to participate in constructive group activities is perhaps one of the better indicators of suitability for the job of being a police officer in the society that we see developing around us today. Past interests and activities of an applicant will often prove to be a far more accurate indicator of the values, attitudes, and overall character of the applicant than any psychological screening test.

**Training:** Most recruit training today pays very little attention to instruction on the ethical standards expected of police officers by their departments and the public whom they serve. In some instances, this lack of attention to ethics is excused on the grounds that (a) there isn't enough time to cover such "minor" matters and (b) one cannot teach someone to be ethical. Neither of these objections is valid. However, this training, to be effective, must be more than a mere review of the code of conduct of the department. Ethics training in police recruit classes must be reality-based and must involve more than just a simple discussion of integrity. The training must be candid and involve a free discussion of the potential problems and pitfalls that challenge police officers on the job. It must include discussion of the temptations that they will face, the stresses of police work, the effects of a career in police on personal life, and related matters.

**Policies and Procedures:** Once officers are on duty with the department, clear and consistent policies and procedures are essential to let these officers know what is expected from them, what the acceptable limits are on their discretion, and what means and methods are or are not permissible in performing the job.

**Supervision:** Supervision, particularly first-line supervision, is a critical element in maintaining proper ethical standards among police officers. Supervisors must (a) believe in the standards set by the department (b) observe them personally, and (c) enforce them consistently and fairly in their departments

**Discipline:** Holding personnel strictly accountable for their actions is the backbone of accountability. But the system of discipline must be rationally based, reasonable, and consistently and fairly administered. Perhaps even more important, the system must not only decree punishment for infractions, but must also provide rewards for positive behaviour.

**Police Culture:** Police work is not just a job; it is a way of life. Much has been written about the influences that the culture of policing has on police officers and police conduct. Innumerable scholars and observers of the police profession have held that, more than any other factor, the attitudes, beliefs, behaviour, and actions of police officers are determined by the working environment within the police organization and on the street. Their reaction to that environment, both good and bad, defines what sociologists like to refer to as the police subculture.

The community of police work and the resultant camaraderie of police officers are important sources of positive support for officers and their families. However, the negative side of this support system can be a misguided sense of interpersonal loyalty that overlooks or even covers up misdeeds and wrongdoing. When officers instinctively tend to focus on protecting their coworkers, rather than on the wrong that has been done, they are abdicating their personal and professional responsibility as peace officers. This is not the role of policing in a democracy, and it suggests problems not only for officers involved but also for the police organization as a whole.

Police organizations should take whatever steps possible to direct loyalty, fidelity, and fellowship into positive efforts to maintain the ethical standards that are so essential to law enforcement today. These efforts are not always easy and may often require major changes in organizational styles as well as management and supervisory practices. The police culture must be recognized as a source for positive reinforcement and support of values and ethics. Ethics becomes an integral part of the police culture when officers understand the role and importance of ethics in their lives and their profession, internalize those roles, and hold their colleagues accountable to the same high ethical standards as they do themselves. Under such a system, all officers become examples to their colleagues.

In summary, the police working environment must be geared to encouraging — and allowing all of its personnel to be examples of the best in the police profession. When the entire organization subscribes to an ethical, value-based system, all officers can serve as role models, both to their colleagues and to the community.

Authorities who have studied the police profession often advise that one of the better ways to accomplish this goal is to transform police departments from the traditionally autocratic paramilitary forces of the past into more democratic organization, broad-based departments in which individual officers' talents and ideas are encouraged and used constructively, and in which management and line functions are working in a compatible and mutually supporting manner. This environment must be based upon mutually accepted, goal-directed efforts that are founded upon a value system that is clearly defined and firmly accepted as a result of the joint endeavours of all members of the department.

*Reference :*
- Beauchamp, T.L. & Childress, J.F. (1994), Principles of biomedical ethics (4*th* ed.), New York: Oxford University press.
- Beauchamp, T.L. & Childress, J.F. (1994), Principles of biomedical ethics (4*th* ed.), New York: Oxford University press.
- Kithcener, K.S. (1984), Intuition, critical evaluation and ethical principles: The foundation for ethical decisions in counseling psychology. The Counselling Psychologist, 12(3), 43-55
- Komives, S.R., Lucas, N., & McMahon, T.R. (1998), Exploring leadership: For college students who want to make a difference. San Francisco: Jossey-Bass.
- Beauchamp, T.L. & Childress, J.F. (1994), Principles of biomedical ethics (4*th* ed.), New York: Oxford University press.
- Ibid
- Kanungo, R.N. & Mendonca, M. (1996), Ethical dimensions of leadership. Thousand Oaks, CA: Sage
- Beauchamp, T.L. & Childress, J.F. (1994), Principles of biomedical ethics (4*th* ed.), New York: Oxford University press.
- Greenleaf, R.K. (1977), Servant leadership: A journey into the nature of legimimate power and greatness, New York, Paulist.
- Gilligan, C (1982), In a different voice: Psychological theory and women's development. Cambridge, MA: Harvard University Press
- Block, P. (1993), Stewarship: choosing service over self-interest. San Francisco: Berret-Koehler.
- Covey, S.R. (1990), Principle-centered leadership, New York: Fireside

- De Pree, M. (1989) *Leadership is an art*, New York: Doubleday
- Kouzes, J J & Posner, B.z. (1995), *The leadership challenge : How to keep getting extraordinary things done in organization* (2$^{nd}$ ed.) San Francisco: Jossey-Bass
- SengeP.M. (1990), *The fifth discipline: The art and practice of the learning organization*, New York: doubleday
- Rawls, J. (1971), *A theory of justice*. Boston: Harvard University Press
- Beauchamp, T.L. & Childress, J.F. (1994), *Principles of biomedical ethics* (4$^{th}$ ed.), New York: Oxford University press.
- Jaska, J.A. & Pritchard, M.S. (1988), *Communication ethics: Methods of analysis*. Belmont, CA: Wadsworth
- Dalla Costa, J. (1998). *The ethical imperative: why moral leadership is good business*. Reading, MA: Addisson-Wesley
- Bass, B.M. & Steidlmeier, P. (1999), *Ethics, character and authentic transformational leadership behaviour*, Leadership Quarterly, 10(2), 181-217
- Beauchamp, T.L. & Childress, J.F. (1994), *Principles of biomedical ethics* (4$^{th}$ ed.), New York: Oxford University press.
- Rost, J.c. (1991) *Leadership for the twenty-first century*, New York: Praeger.
- *Statement of Values of the Alexandria, Virginia, Police Department*.
- Edward A. Thibault, *The Blue Milieu: Police as a Vocational Subculture*, in John W. Bizzack, Ed., Issues in Policing: New Perspectives, Autumn House Publishing,Lexington, KY.
- Bushey,Keith.D,*Setting Ethics Standards Early*,in Police Chief Volume LXVII,No :8 ,IACP, USA

# MEDICAL TOURISM: A NEW HORIZON

Medical or Health tourism has become a common form of vacationing, and covers a broad spectrum of medical services. It mixes leisure, fun and relaxation together with wellness and healthcare. The idea of the health holiday is to offer an opportunity to get away from the daily routine into more relaxed surroundings, to enjoy being close to the beach and the mountains in salubrious climate. At the same time one is able to receive an orientation that will help improve life in terms of health and general well being. It is like rejuvenation and a clean - up process on all levels - physical, mental and emotional.

What's called medical tourism – patients going to a different country for either urgent or elective medical procedures – is fast becoming a worldwide, multibillion-dollar industry. The reasons patients travel for treatment vary. Many medical tourists from the United States are seeking treatment at a quarter or sometimes even a tenth of the cost at home. From Canada, it is often people who are frustrated by long waiting times. From Great Britain, the patient can't wait for treatment by the National Health

Service but also can't afford to see a physician in private practice. For others, becoming a medical tourist is a chance to combine a tropical vacation with elective or plastic surgery. And more patients are coming from poorer countries such as Bangladesh where treatment may not be available.

Medical tourism is actually thousands of years old. In ancient Greece, pilgrims and patients were coming from all over the Mediterranean to the sanctuary of the healing god "Asklepios" at Epidaurus. In Roman Britain, patients took the waters at a shrine at Bath, a practice that continued for 2,000 years. Since the 18th century, wealthy Europeans travelled to spas scattered all the way from Germany to the Nile. Countries that actively promote medical tourism include Cuba, Costa Rica, Hungary, India, Israel, Jordan, Lithuania, Malaysia and Thailand. Belgium, Poland and Singapore are now entering the field. South Africa specializes in medical safaris-visit the country for a safari, with a stopover for plastic surgery, a nose job and a chance to see lions and elephants.

The royal palaces of the erstwhile Indian Maharajas were the nurturing grounds for the discovery and practice of natural therapies of holistic well being. Human values, thoughts, ideas have, since then, undergone a paradigm shift of sorts, but nature has not yielded. Indeed, ancient preparations and applications have filtered down the centuries to become a part of the Indian cultural legacy.However what is less dwelt upon and is indeed very interesting is how the pathways of seemingly different therapy's like ayurveda and aromatherapy meander through and cross onto each other, so as to forge together an exuberant world of health and happiness.

In fact, the science of Ayurveda has been practiced in

India for over 10,000 years. Ayurveda is composed of two Sanskrit words: Ayur meaning life and Veda meaning knowledge. Together they mean knowledge of life or the science of divine healing.

Steeped in tradition and scientific thought, Vedic philosophy has been a great influence not merely within India, but also in different parts of the world. Its far reaching impact can be understood completely when one whole heartedly integrates the body, mind and soul with the environment, as the microcosm of the self is a mere reflection of the macrocosm, the universe that surrounds us. Various holistic techniques for the enlightenment and enrichment of the self have emerged from Vedic thought.

The oldest surviving medical system of the world, Ayurveda maintains a perfect and harmonious balance in human existence, espousing the fact that we are spirits manifested as humans, experiencing existence. Ayurveda blends science & philosophy while balancing mental, physical, spiritual and emotional facets of a being.Following an Ayurvedic lifestyle, counteracting disease by massage, Yoga, cleansing and detoxification and natural verbal remedies are considered the stepping stones for physical and mental being.

Yoga can be effectively used to fight deadly diseases such as cancer after being integrated with allopathic medicine. A patient visualizes the white blood cells attacking and inning over the irregularly shaped cancer cells, in a technique called 'Yoga Nidra', which trains the subconscious mind in the battle against cancer. This method is supported by the reputed Regional Cancer centre (M N J Institute of Oncology, Red Hills, Hyderabad) and the Apollo Cancer Centre, Chennai.

Medical Tourism refers to the movement of consumers

to the country providing the service for diagnosis and treatment. During the past few years, the number of people going out of their home country to consume health services have significantly increased. The size of this market is estimated to be $40 billion based on a Saudi Report in 2000. During the past four years, the market grew at a whopping rate of 20-30% and is expected to grow further. Considering this growth the current market size is estimated to be $100 billion. Medical Tourism industry offers tremendous potential for the developing countries because of their low-cost advantage. The advantages of medical tourism include improvement in export earnings and healthcare infrastructure. No doubt a lot of countries are fighting for a share of the market. In order to realize the full potential of the industry. it is imperative for these countries to develop a strategic plan for coordinating various industry players - the medical practitioners, private hospitals, policy makers, hotels, transportation services and tour operators.

Medical tourism can be broadly defined as provision of 'cost effective' private medical care in collaboration with the tourism industry for patients needing any forms of specialized treatment. This process is being facilitated by the corporate sector involved in medical care as well as the tourism industry -both private and public.

India is considered the leading country promoting medical tourism and now it is moving into a new area of "medical outsourcing," where subcontractors provide services to the overburdened medical care systems in western countries.

India's National Health Policy declares that treatment of foreign patients is legally an "export" and deemed "eligible for all fiscal incentives extended to export earnings." Government and private sector studies in India estimate that medical tourism could bring between $1 billion and $2 billion US into the country by 2012. The reports estimate that the numer of medical tourists to India is growing by 30 per cent a year.

India's top-rated education system is not only churning out computer programmers and engineers, but an estimated 20,000 to 30,000 doctors and nurses each year. Among the top medical corporations in India serving medical tourists Apollo Hospital Enterprises is the largest and has treated an estimated 60,000 patients between 2001 and spring 2004. It is Apollo that is aggressively moving into medical outsourcing. Apollo already provides overnight computer services for U.S. insurance companies and hospitals as well as working with big pharmaceutical corporations with drug trials. Dr. Prathap C. Reddy, the chairman of the company, began negotiations in the spring of 2004 with Britain's National Health Service to work as a subcontractor, to do operations and medical tests for patients at a fraction of the cost in Britain for either government or private care.

Apollo's business began to grow in the 1990s, with the deregulation of the Indian economy, which drastically cut the bureaucratic barriers to expansion and made it easier to import the most modern medical equipment. The first patients were Indian expatriates who returned home for treatment; major investment houses followed with money and then patients from Europe, the Middle East and Canada began to arrive. Apollo now has 37 hospitals, with about 7,000 beds. The company has now joint venture hospitals in Kuwait, Sri Lanka and Nigeria.

Western patients usually get a package deal that includes flights, transfers, hotels, treatment and often a post-operative vacation.

Apollo has also expanded its services to millions of poor

Indians. It has set aside free beds for those who can't afford care, has set up a trust fund and is pioneering remote, satellite-linked telemedicine across India.

**The downsides of medical tourism**

Experts have identified a number of problems with medical tourism
- Government and basic medical insurance, and sometimes extended medical insurance, often does not pay for the medical procedure, meaning the patient has to pay cash.
- There is little follow-up care. The patient usually is in hospital for only a few days, and then goes on the vacation portion of the trip or returns home. Complications, side-effects and post-operative care are then the responsibility of the medicalcare system in the patients' home country.
- Most of the countries that offer medical tourism have weak malpractice laws, so patient has little recourse to local courts or medical boards if something goes wrong.
- There are growing accusations that profitable, private-sector medical tourism is drawing medical resources and personnel away from the local population, although some medical organizations that market to outside tourists are taking steps to improve local service.

India has one of the best qualified professionals in each and every field, and this fact has now been realized the world over. Regarding medical facilities India has the most competent doctors and world class medical facilities. With most competitive charges for treatment, India is a very lucrative destination for people wanting to undergo treatment of certain medical problems who do not need immediate emergency treatment.

If medical tourism has existed for thousands of years. why has it begun to grow so rapidly only in the recent past? The reason is in the intersection of two factors. On one side, the cost of high-speed air travel has been dropping and is now within the grasp of all but the poorest of the developed world. Even as air travel costs have dropped, the costs of healthcare in the developed world have climbed steadily. Capitalizing on this, a number of third-world countries have built world-class medical facilities. Generally, these hospitals started out by catering to expatriates from rich Western countries and emigrants to the West who could combine medical treatment with a trip home. As these hospitals have established their reputations, many have sought to market themselves to all citizens of the developed world and to make themselves attractive to foreigners. For example, Wockhardt Hospital in Bangalore has succeeded in forming an alliance with Harvard Medical Alliance, a subsidiary of the Harvard Medical School, and in joining the American Blue Cross Blue Shield network. Bumrungrad Hospital in Bangkok, Thailand, which offers its website in fifteen languages and provides travel packages with online quotes, is a member of Joint Commission Resources, an international accreditation organization. In addition, specialized travel agencies have arisen to offer vacation/ operation packages for clients who would like to take in a safari with their South African facelift or a trip to the Taj Mahal to try out their new hip joint. Like companies who outsource their call centers and software development to India and other countries, the main attraction of outsourcing one's medical treatment is cost. The cost of labor at a hospital in India, Thailand or South Africa is only a fraction of the cost in the United States. Cost is by far the most significant driver of this trend.

From less than *10,000* patients visiting India for medical

treatment five years ago, the medical tourism market in India is worth US$ 333 million, with about *100,000* foreign patients coming in every year. Economic incentives have been introduced towards upgrading existing infrastructure to make India a global health care destination. These include tax sops to financial institutions lending to private groups setting up hospitals with 100 or more beds, and an increase in the rate of depreciation from 25 per cent to 40 per cent for life-saving medical equipment. State governments, private hospital groups, and even travel agencies have all caught on to the trend.

- Leading Indian travel houses like Sita and Kuoni have launched tie-ups with overseasplayers that focus on medical tourism.
- Some state government like Karnataka is setting up Bangalore International Health City Corporation, which will cater to international patients for a wide variety of health careproducts and treatments.
- The Asian Heart Institute at Mumbai's Bandra-Kurla Complex, offers state-of-the art facilities for all types of heart complications.

# IDENTITY TOURISM

With a rapidly evolving tourism scenario, the traveller's motive to venture out has also undergone rapid change, ranging from varying motives for leisure to a need for the search for identity. One of the evident consequences of tourism is defying the monotony of routine life and seeking out an "authentic" experience. Wang (1999) indicates that tourists are not only searching for the "Other", but are also on a quest for self-identity and that tourism is a vessel for self discovery. Bandyopadhyay (2008) has indicated that identity is essentially an individual notion. Regarding touristic experiences, "both remembering and forgetting also underlie a "subjective sense of identity" that is only inadequately reproduced in language.

The identity concept is central to the study of tourism. Tourism marketer's have created, reaffirmed and altered cultural, regional, national, ethnic, gender identities for tourists.

**Objective:**

The aim of this study is to enhance the understanding of the role played by personal identity in tourism and vice versa. A narrative approach was used involving two interviews with 10 participants. The first interview was a travel life history, in which participants recalled all of their holidays throughout the course of their lives. The second interview explored interviewees' views and opinions on the environment and travel. This study therefore questions the assumption that behaviour change can be effectively managed given individuals' needs to negotiate a variety of identity interests.

**Aim and objectives**

The aim of this research is to enhance the understanding of the role played by personal identity in tourism mobility. This will be achieved through the following objectives:
- To examine travel 'life histories' as mechanisms to explore identity formation and resultant identity markers in a tourism context.
- To explore the ways in which identity may influence a person's evolving tourist travel behaviour.
- To analyse the manner in which home identities are presented in relation to away identities.
- To analyse how the identities of people embedded in highly mobile lifestyles are constructed or negotiated in the light of current debates on climate change.

One significant element which plays a role in travel behaviour is identity. Desforges (2000) suggests that identity issues lie at the heart of our desire for travel. Highly mobile lifestyles are currently viewed as a positive identity marker. As outlined by Urry (2012), high mobility is associated with a high degree of 'meetingness', i.e., an individual's standing in society is reflected in mobility patterns, which ultimately necessitates air travel. This is also demonstrated through airlines' use of frequent flyer programmes which "reward and thus increase interest in mobility" (Gössling and Nilsson 2010, p. 242). It could be argued that such marketing strategies hold some responsibility for the status implied in highly mobile lifestyles through their inclusion of VIP lounges for members and add to the status attached to exotic international tourism. Current literature relating to identities and tourism tends to focus on either 'finding yourself' through travel (e.g. Fullagar 2002; Noy 2004a) or using travel as a symbol of status (e.g. Thurlow and Jaworski 2006; Urry 2012).

Desforges (2000) suggests that understanding identity can give insight into tourism consumption because, by understanding the person and their needs and desires, it could be possible to predict their future travel behaviour. If the tourism identity processes an individual goes through could be understood, it might be possible to influence desired identities and, consequently, travel behaviour.

## Transformation of Self

*We are, not what we are, but what we make of ourselves. It would not be true to say that the self is regarded as entirely empty of content, for there are psychological processes of self-formation, and psychological needs, which provide the parameters for the reorganized self. Otherwise, however, what the individual becomes is dependent on the reconstructive endeavours in which he or she engages. These are far more than just "getting to know oneself? better: self-understanding is subordinated to the more inclusive and fundamental aim of building/rebuilding a coherent and rewarding sense of identity. The involvement of such reflexivity with social and psychological research is striking, and a pervasive feature of the therapeutic outlook advocated* (Giddens, 1991, p. 75).

The idea of "personhood" in tourism studies, such as identity, subjectivity, and the self, are supplemented in this paper through an empirical approach to identity and tourism consumption patterns. Anthony Giddens' analysis of contemporary self-identity is adopted as a research strategy for analysing "travel biographies". In-depth interviews with tourists will lead to an understanding of which tourism consumption is mobilized for self-identity.

Therefore, a narrative approach was used to explore the travel life histories of 24 participants. A second interview examined how interviewees viewed their identities and tourism activity in the light of environmental debates and concerns

## Understanding identity and the self

Without prior knowledge of the existing literature, it would be easy to suggest that many of the terms, such as 'self-concept', 'self-image', 'self-identity' and others listed below, are the same concept but phrased differently (e.g. Ashmore and Jussim 1997). It is only after consulting various sources that the distinctions, some of which are negligible, become apparent. On the other hand, many concepts and theories are intertwined and overlap in some way (Seigel 2005).

### *Self-concept*

'Self-concept' is an important term in identity literature; in layman's terms, it is how individuals see and describe themselves. Onkvisit and Shaw (1987, p.14) state that an individual's self-concept refers to: "the ideas and feelings that he has about himself in relation to others in a socially determined frame of reference." They argue that individuals are constantly assessing their environment and objects within this environment. In their discussion, they assert that individuals may consider themselves as an object for assessment within the environment. Self-concept is based on an assessment of how individuals see themselves and, additionally, their perception of how other people view them "through the eyes of other people ... [taking] into account their behaviour, attitudes and approval among other things" (Onkvisit and Shaw 1987, p.14). Hogg and Terry (2000) also affirm that self-concept is defined through group membership and the acknowledgement of the necessary characteristics for membership of the group in question.

Gecas (1982) asserts that self-concept can be approached from two perspectives within social psychology; one has roots in sociology and the other is rooted in psychology. The sociological perspective looks at predecessors of self-concept and searches for instances of these within social interactions. Psychology, on the other hand, looks at behavioural-related consequences of self-conceptions. Both perspectives are important for this research. An explanation of self-concept is provided by Gecas (1982), who makes clear the distinction between 'self' and 'self-concept'. He explains that a self-concept is the result of an individual reflexively assessing themselves in terms of 'I' and 'me'. The resultant self-concept is thus "the concept the individual has of himself as a physical, social and spiritual or moral being" (Gecas 1982, p.3). The 'I' and 'me' that Gecas (1982) refers to are based on William James' explanation of the self in 1892. James was one of the forefathers of American psychology and his work on the self is deemed relevant many years later (e.g. Goffman 1959; Gecas 1982; Belk 1988; Markus and Kitayama 1991; McAdams 1993). Holstein and Gubrium (2000) explain that 'I' is the awareness of self's point of origin and 'me' is the object of that sense of awareness.

'Self-image' is a term which is hard to distinguish from 'self-concept'; in fact, Graeff (1996) uses the terms interchangeably. However, Fein and Spencer (1997) make a suggestion that 'self-concept' was a common term up to 20 years prior to their research but, at the time they went to press, authors were referring to 'self-image'. Davies (1996) suggests that the levels of our self-esteem can be indicated through the image of ourselves that we present to others. She also proposes that our self-image is influenced not only by self-esteem but by the psychological impacts of our relationships with our parents, as well as past experiences we may have had. Self-esteem is an important term. To consider when looking at self and identities. Self-esteem is essentially the result of an individual's evaluation of their self-concept and is thought to have a motivational significance (Gecas 1982).

Bannister and Hogg (2004) even go as far as suggesting that self-esteem is thought to be one of the most significant factors motivating consumer decisions. They also highlight that self-esteem can be enhanced by particular consumption choices and that products will be rejected or considered because of their perceived contribution to increasing self-esteem.

Hogg and Abrams (1988) propose that self-concept could be placed on a continuum, ranging from exclusively social to exclusively personal identity, and that the social setting in which the individual is placed at a certain moment in time will dictate which self-concept is the most prominent.

**Personal identity**

Hogg and Abrams (1988) cite Gergen (1971) to describe the elements that can construct an individual's identity.

They state that personal identity consists of descriptions of self that are specific and personal to the individual in question and usually contain descriptions of attributes. They state that personal identity refers to "idiosyncratic descriptions of self which are essentially tied to and emerge from close and enduringinterpersonal relationships" (Hogg and Abrams 1988, p.25). Personal identity is thus not only an individual matter but is also closely tied to others. Layder (2004) also discusses personal identity in terms of relationships with others. He states that personal identity is made up of the distinctive elements that make a person unique and that it is more than physical characteristics; it is "a centre of awareness, emotional needs and desires, in terms of which an individual reflects and acts upon his or her social circumstances.

Turner (1982) asserts that an individual's personal identity will alter, depending on the context of the groups they find themselves in. This is in line with Goffman's (1959) idea of performing an identity for a certain audience. This is because an individual's personal identity is very closely related to their social identity; one influences the other (i.e. one's personal identity helps form one's social identity and vice versa) and both are likely to change with each new circumstance. Turner (1982, p.20) goes on to further state that "social behaviour, therefore, should presumably tend to display some characteristic variation as the locus of cognitive control is switched from personal to social identity", which reflect his belief that an identity can adapt or morph depending on the situation. For example, an individual's behaviour may change depending on whether they are surrounded by work colleagues or lifelong friends, with whom they can be their 'real' self. This is confirmed by Turner et al. (2006, p.16) who re-assert the fact that identity can and will vary.

*Identity and tourism research*

At present, the literature relating to identity and tourism tends to focus on identity issues, such as 'finding yourself' through travel. For example, Noy's (2004a) study of Israeli backpackers' narratives demonstrates how they used tourism to construct their identity; they had returned from their trips 'changed' people. These holidays are considered to be 'fateful moments' in the lives of the backpackers. Several authors have discussed tourism as moments of change, in terms of Heidegger's existential authenticity (see: Wang 1999; Steiner and Reisinger 2006; Brown 2013). Bruner (1991, p.239) even acknowledges that tourist brochures use this element of finding oneself as a selling point "... a trip to remember for a lifetime and [the tourist] will return refreshed and renewed, as a new and different person." However, his research questions whether the tourist self is changed and argues that the native self is the one who experiences the greater change through contact with culturally different and more developed tourists. This is revealed in research conducted by Abbott Cone (1995). She demonstrates how two Mayan women have created new identities for themselves through the catalyst of contact with Western tourists. Their exposure to Western values has given them a new group to use as a reference point and has led them to break away from the traditional values of their culture. As discussed earlier in the chapter, an understanding of self and one's own identity comes from a discovery of 'other' (Burke 2001). In this way tourism can be seen to be linked to identity as it is by nature a discovery of the 'other' and provides opportunity for self-reflection (Galani-Moutafi 2000). Cohen (2010), in opposition to Bruner, proposes that it might be unrealistic to use travel to 'find yourself' because the self is constantly evolving and changing anyway. In this way, the lifestyle travellers of Cohen's research are simply acting out the expected discourse of finding themselves.

The other identity and tourism perspective is that discussed by Thurlow and Jaworski (2006) and relates to using travel to affirm identities. These authors discuss the use of frequent flyer programmes to create or reinforce status; "regular customers are declared 'elite' and ... this status is then fabricated and regulated" (Thurlow and Jaworski 2006, p.100). The authors, although aware of the marketing techniques used by airlines in the creation of the status associated with frequent flyer programmes, admit to falling victim to their ploys themselves:

"we both therefore feel a certain need to acknowledge the guilty pleasure, or childlike triumph, we feel in marching to the front of check-in queues, being sequestered from the bustle of the terminal concourse, and sidestepping the throngs when boarding an aeroplane" (Thurlow and Jaworski 2006, p.101).

The identity perspective here is that of frequent flyer programmes allowing for a presentation of a higher social status, therefore, members are treated as 'elite'. This thesis approaches identity and travel from a slightly different angle; it considers the impact of existing identities on the desire to travel rather than identities purely being created through travel.

An additional identity perspective within the tourism literature involves the idea of liminality. Tourist spaces are often viewed as liminal places because the tourist is free to escape the norms of their everyday life and adopt temporary identities while on holiday (Boissevain 1996). It is thought that when they return from the holiday they will revert back to their 'old' identity and behaviour

(Turner 1982). Kim and Jamal (2007) also assert that tourism can be used as a means to escape the rules of everyday norms. This would potentially allow tourists to perform 'green' identities at home yet continue to undertake activities such as flying.

Identity is important to tourism research because, as seen from these examples, travel is thought to have the ability to change people. For many, holidays play an important part in who they are; memories are not always just stored away (Trauer and Ryan 2005; Heimtun 2007; Heimtun and Jordan 2011), they can be used to shape the future self of the traveller. This finding has been widely discussed in the literature (Bruner 1991; Desforges 2000; Fullegar 2002; Noy 2004a; Thurlow and Jaworski 2006). Wearing and Wearing (2001) add depth to this argument by acknowledging that existing selves are 'taken on holiday' and home again and that the identity of the tourist is embedded in their tourism experience in an iterative process. They view the relationship between tourism and identity as a construction and reconstruction of the self through tourist experiences.

This research investigates identity from a different angle; whether who we are affects our touristic behaviour and mobility. This is connected to the existing research on tourism and identity, as it forms part of the continuous spiral of identity formation; i.e., previous research suggests that travel is transformative (Brown 2009); this research suggests that 'self' influences travel in the first place (whilst also acknowledging the previous point). Thus, identity formation in regard to tourism experiences is an iterative process, i.e., an identity is formed, which may influence holiday choices; holiday experiences may then shape identity, and the process therefore repeats itself. This process is on-going and identities are never static (Gillespie 2007).

Research undertaken by Becken (2007) indicates that tourists see travel as part of their identity. Their holidays have a great meaning to them and help them to understand their position in society. In addition, using incentives, such as frequent flyer programmes 37 that play on people's identities or desired identities, can shape travel patterns, as is also the case with travel brochures, which create an iterative and self-referencing process.

Harrison (2003) explores the meaning that tourists place on their travel. Similarly to this study she also uses a narrative approach to understand tourists travel biographies. She provides four major conclusions on the meaning of tourists' travel: tourists use travel as a means for intimacy and connection to one another; as a method of expressing their personal values; some saw travel as a way to understand 'home'; and also travelled in order to make sense of a globalised world. Harrison's study demonstrates that using a tourist's narrative it is possible to understand the motivations of their travel and the meaning they place on it. However, I feel that there is also scope for more work in this area in order to further understand the person behind the travel.

John Urry must be seen as one of the leaders in the field of mobilities studies. He has created several definitions of types of mobilities; the following are taken from Larsen et al. (2006, p.56) but are derived from Urry's earlier work (see also Urry 2002; 2003):

- **Physical travel** – the movement of people for reasons that include work, leisure, family life, pleasure, migration and escape. This form of mobility stems from the need to be in the same place as specific other people, or to physically experience specific locations or events. Physical proximity is necessary.

**Physical movement** – of objects to/from producers, consumers and retailers. This mobility is linked to consumption.

**Imaginative travel** - to 'elsewhere' through various forms of media (memories, text messages, images, television and films). Urry claims that this "will often substitute for physical transport." The example used is football fans who watch away matches whilst at home or at the pub, instead of attending live matches. This has been made possible through the growth of television ownership and the broadcasting of live matches. However, it is arguable whether it could ever be a complete substitute. Imaginative travel has, in some cases, increased physical travel through producing or enhancing the desire to visit destinations that have been used in films or television series. This is known in the literature as 'media pilgrimage' and narrows the distance between reality and fantasy (Couldry 2005). The anticipation phase of tourism is also allied to imaginative travel, as people explore and plan potential holiday options.

**Virtual travel** – on the internet, takes place in real time. It reduces the need for physical movement in order to partake in activities, such as banking or shopping. Urry presents the argument of some authors who suggest that this could reduce traditional tourism; however, it is very difficult to see how the internet could be an adequate substitute for the sensations experienced by all of the senses whilst on holiday. Examples given were Las Vegas and race tracks, which are very specific activities. I believe that, perhaps, only hardened gamblers would see this as a good substitute, unlike those who travel for the 'complete experience'. Having said that, the complete tourism experience is phased. A considerable amount of time can be spent anticipating and imagining and the web is often used to explore a destination before we get there.

**Communicative travel** – is through messages sent person-to-person through various methods, such as greetings cards, telephones, emails, and instant messages etc. This form of mobility also allows the transportation of documents and images. The introduction of new technologies allows for communication whilst the person is undertaking physical travel – particularly evidenced by the 'new' travel blogging trend.

**Findings:**
- Identities play a major part in travel behaviour and decisions.
- Identities are contextual and can override one another at certain times.
- Tourism generates significant cultural change, which in turn influences youths' past, present, and future perceptions of their community and culture, consequently their identities.

**References:**
1. Babbie, E. (2009). The practice of social research. (12th ed.). Belmont, CA: Wadsworth Publishing.
2. Bandyopadhyay, R. (2008). Nostalgia, identity and tourism: Bollywood in the Indian diaspora. Journal of Tourism and Cultural Change, 6(2), 79-100.
3. Bandyopadhyay, R., Morais, D., & Chick, G. (2008).Religion and identity in India?s heritage tourism. Annals of Tourism Research, 35(3), 790-808.
4. Bærenholdt, J. O., Haldrup, M., Larsen, J., & Urry, J. (2004). Performing tourist places.Aldershot, Hants: Ashgate.
5. Bolla, P. (1990).Media images of women and leisure:An

analysis of magazine advertisements, 1964-87. Leisure Studies, 9(3), 241-252.
6. Bryant, J., & Lasky, B. (2007). A researcher?s tale: Dealing with epistemological divergence. Qualitative Research in Organizations and Management, 2(3), p. 179-193.
7. Callahan, R. (1998). Ethnic politics and tourism: A British case study. Annals of Tourism Research, 25(4),818-836.
8. Calas, M., & Smircich, L. (1999). Past postmodernism? Reflections and tentative directions. Academy of Management Review, 24(4), 649-671.
9. Cano, L., & Mysyk, A. (2004).Cultural tourism, the state, and Day of the Dead. Annals of Tourism Research, 31(4), 879-898.
10. Chhabra, D., Healy, R., & Stills, E. (2003). Staged authenticity and heritage tourism. Annals of Tourism Research, 30(3), 702-719.

# MIND AND MUSIC

*Whether its just entertainment, a cultural expression or religious inspiration, music is part of everyone's life. Music has been found to have a profound effect on our physiological and psychological well-being.*

The courage to create brings many challenges : self-doubt, self-judgement low self-esteem etc/:and with this come unavoidable experiences of stress.

Music therapy interventions can be designed to manage stress, alleviate pain, promote wellness, express feelings, enhance memory, improve communication and promote physical rehabilitation. Music has the power to explore the realms that cannot be accessed with words.

The Indian theory of emotions has been usually associated with a literary appreciation of the theory of "Rasa" (aesthetic emotion) based on Hindu psychology. The study focuses on an analysis of Rasa therapy for the rejuvenation of the mind.

The nine "Rasas" to be demonstrated correspond to nine emotional conditions.

- Sringara (erotic)
- Hasya (humorous)
- Karuna (pathetic)
- Roudra (furious)

- *Veera (valorous)*
- *Bhayanaka (fearful)*
- *Beebhatra (odious)*
- *Adbhuta (wonderous)*
- *Santa (peaceful)*

The paper will involve a depiction of these nine raasas in music and how moods can be attributed to them. The moods created do depend on the notes and their inter-relations.

*The second part of the paper will highlight the relationship of "ragas" to human mind.* "Raagas" are very detailed melodic modes used in Indian classical music traditionally based on an intricate vedic philosophy of sound.

William Congreve wrote:
"Music hath charms to soothe the savage breast,
To soften rocks, or bend a knotted oak,
I have read that things inanimate moved,
And as with living souls have been informed,
By magic numbers and persuasive sound."

Music is the manifestation of human spirit, similar to language. Its greatest practitioners have conveyed to mankind things not possible to say in any other language. Whether it is entertainment, a cultural expression or religious inspiration, music is part of everyone's life. Music has been found to have a profound effect on our physiological and psychological well being.

## Music Therapy:

The courage to create ushers in many challenges – self doubt, low self-esteem etc: and with this come unavoidable experiences of stress. Music has the power to explore the realms that can not be accessed with words. Music therapy is now being increasingly used the world over as a complementary tool to address several ailments with remarkable results. The Joint National Committee, USA in its 7th report listed music as one of the factors that significantly lowers stress levels.

Reports indicate that there is a definite connection between music and academic achievement. The music that makes the foot tap, the fingers snap and the pulse quicken stirs the brain at is most fundamental levels, suggesting that scientists one day may be able to return damaged minds by exploiting rhythm, harmony and melody, according to new research .Exploring the neurobiology of music, researchers discovered direct evidence that music stimulates specific regions of the brain responsible for memory, motor control, timing and language. For the first time, researchers also have located specific areas of mental activity linked to emotional responses to music.

The latest findings, presented at a meeting of the Society for Neuroscience in Los Angeles, underscore how music as an almost universal language of mood, emotion and desire , orchestrates a wide variety of neural systems to cast its evocative spell.  "Undeniably, there is a biology of music," said Harvard University Medical School neurobiologist Mark Jude Tramo.  "There is no question that there is specialization within the human brain for the processing of music. Music is biologically part of human life, just as music is aesthetically part of human life."

Over all, music seems to involve the brain at almost every level. Even allowing for cultural differences in musical tastes, the researchers found evidence of music's remarkable power to affect neural activity no matter where they look in the brain, from primitive regions in all animals to more recently evolved regions thought to be distinctively human. Music exists in every culture, and infants have excellent musical abilities that cannot be explained by learning. Mothers everywhere sing to their infants because babies understand it. Music seems to be part of our biological heritage

From enhancing concentration and memory to dealing with diabetics as well as boosting ones immunity, music therapy lends its healing touch. The passive form of music therapy, (listening) has a beneficial effect in almost all ailments whereas the active form, (participating) is especially helpful for neurological problems. Music integrates mind, body and spirit and provide opportunities for self-expression.

Dr.Nishindra Kinjalk lists some ailments and the corresponding ragas which may benefit patients :

Depression : Komal Rishabh Asawari (day) and Shankara (night)

Anxiety : Nat Bhairav (day) and Sohni (night)

Parkinson's : Bhatiyar (day) and Yamen (night)

Acidity : Bairagi (day) and Bhoopali (night)

Hypertension and Heart Problem : Todi (day) and Pooriya Kalyan (night)

Labour pains : Jaunpuri (day), Hameer (evening) and Abhogi (late night)

Stroke : Ramkali (day) and Gorakh Kalyan (night)

Asthma : Nilambari (day), Megh (night) and Bharavi (any time)

**Rasa :**

The Indian theory of emotions has been usually associated with a literary appreciation of the theory of "Rasa", based on Hindu psychology. Though raga itself is identified with emotion, in most of the current literature, it is both emotional behaviour and more; it is an awareness of the totality of the emotional situation. It is a detached observance of such a condition of mind and body.

"The experience of rasa is absolute and is known only by empathy....that is to say, by entering into, feeling the permanent motif". "Delightful or disgusting, exalted or lowly, obscure or refined, actual or imagery, there is no subject that can not evoke rasa in man". While finally rasa is a contemplative state of mind, there are said to be nine rasas corresponding to nine emotional conditions : sringara (erotic), hasya (humorous), karuna (pathetic), roudra (furious), veera (valorous), bhayanaka (fearful), beebhatsa (odious), adbhuta (wonderous) and santa (peaceful).

Right from very ancient days attempts have been made to relate these specific rasas to music. Bharata said, for instance, the ethos of a jati depends on the dominant note in it : madhyama – humorous, panchama – erotic, shadja – valorous, rishabha – furious, and so on. Sarangadeva (13th cent.) says that shadja and rishaba should be used for veera (valorous), dhaivata for beebhatsa (odious) and bhayanaka (fearful), gandhara and nishada for karuna (pathetic), panchama and madhyama for hasya (humorous).

In Indian music, raga-bhava is the expressive aspect that is to be experienced in the performance of a raga. The rasa experience, brought about by the perception of the raga-bhava has the potential to effect an experience in the listener tantamount to a divine revelation.

### Raaga:

A Raga is a melodic concept and has a traditionally defined grammar. It is possible to have many kinds of compositions in a raga; conversely any type of composition is generally possible in a variety of ragas. In our own times musicians have attributed moods to ragas. During the last few centuries, it was customary to anthropomorphize ragas in the form of demigods and celectial nymphs. Melodies of Khamaj type, some say, are erotic, and those with ma-dha

(F#-Ab) combinations express pathos and lassitude. Of course, there is not much doubt that the moods created do depend on the notes used and their interrelations, for the state of mind aroused by a set of consonant tones is surely different from that due to dissonant ones.

Very recently some experiments on current scientific lines were conducted by measuring the responses to defined phrases of a few ragas. It was found that they did produce fairly similar moods in all the listeners participating in the experiment, as instanced below.

*Kafi* : very effective, humid, cool, soothing, light (not dense), deep; does not agitate.

*Misra Mand* : pleasing, gay, refreshing, light, sweet; deep; does not agitate; has no feeling of novelty.

*Pooriya Dhanasri* : sweet, colourful, deep, heavy, weary; reflects stability; cloudy; sacred; has no vitality.

*Ragesri* : sweet, soothing, deep, weary, dark; no novelty and is inflexible; stable and calm.

In another set of studies, the relations of a few ragas to their rasas were studied using present techniques in behavioural psychology, semantics, statistics and computerization. As an example ; raga bhairav of Hindustani music had veera (courageous) bhayanaka (fearful) santa (tranquil) and rasas (mental state). It was associated with autumn, early morning and white colour. These responses tally very well indeed with our ancient introspective descriptions of the raga : this is all the more significant as most of those who took part in the experiment were ignorant of our canonical music.

Closely linked with the ethos of a raga is its association with the seasons of the year and the time of the day, specially in Hindustani music. (South Indian Music, however, has no such traditions, except for a small number of melodic types). For example, the North Indian Basant and Bahar are of spring time, Malhar is of the rainy season; indeed this raga is famous for its magical powers. It is believed that rains can be made to pour down by singing it. Once the court musicians of Akbar, a famous emperor of India became jealous of Tansen's (the court musician) eminence and friendship with the Emperor. To destroy him they played a ruse and suggested to Akbar that he command Tansen to sing raga Deepak (Melody of Lights), knowing full well that it would burn him up. Not aware of such consequences, the Emperor requested the great singer to sing to him Raga Deepak. The royal command could not be disobeyed; and so Tansen began to sing the raga. One by one the lamps in the palace courtyard, where he was performing began to light up by themselves. As the music proceeded, the heat started to consume his body. The stupefied king did not know of a way of stopping this slow but sure death. Then someone thought of Tansen's lady who was herself a great musician. She was immediately informed of the tragic situation. On hearing of the danger to her lover, she began to sing raga Malhar and surely the rains came, drenching Tansen and saving his life.

Indian art, whether it be painting, poetry, dance or music has a characteristically inward quality. This is a manifestation of the bias and world-view of this culture. The nature of creation and its forces are not felt and thought about commencing at the point of material phenomena. Indian thought at its deepest, affirms that mind and matter are rather different grades of the same energy, different organizations of one conscious Force of Existence. Hence the external and its imitation have had little place in our art. The outside is only a projection of this "Force of Existence", experienced within and "beauty does not arise from the subject of a work of art, but from the necessity that has been felt of representing that subject". That is why programmatic music is not considered of really deep quality and it is a recent occurrence in the country, specially with the ballet and the films. Imitations of thunder and the ripple of water is not great music, just as realistic photographic painting is not great art. The languor of rains after an Indian summer is what Malhar expresses but not the patter of drops on a tin roof!

Music, as well as being the most dispensable of arts, is probably the hardest to throw off. Just as memories and landscapes eventually emerge to make emotional claims upon us, music comes uninvited. And stays. It is the lure of place, the call to belong. So the essential purpose of Music would be to dynamically orient the body and mind in relation to the environment, both consciously and unconsciously. Thus the integrated, experiential nature of music makes it a profound and unique way of knowing, being and being well.

*References:*
- Ashton, R., (Ed), Music : East and West (Indian Council for Cultural Relations, New Delhi, 1966). A comparative study of Indian and Western Music
- Danielou, A., The Ragas of North Indian Music (Munshi Ram Monoharlal Delhi) Notations (staff) of Hindustani ragas.
- Goswami, O., The story of Indian Music (Asia, Bombay, 1957). General.
- Sambamoorthy, P., History of Indian Music (Indian Music Publ. Hs., Madras, 1960). Mainly South Indian.
- Subba Rao, T.V., Studies in Indian Music (Asia, 1965). Collected essays on Karnatak Music.

# MUSIC TOURISM :
# THE INNOVATIVE EDGE

Tourism needs innovation as a reaction to the dynamics of the cultural-tourism market. Many Indian regions exhibit valuable cultural-tourism capabilities, which have to be "brought alive". The tourism scenario is undergoing drastic changes and is frequently confronted with new challenges. One dimension of the change can be identified as the emergence of new forms of tourism, characterized by the tendency to depart from mass tourism. Innovative attempts gain new strategic value when viewed from a perspective that values experience as an important new attribute. Such a perspective has significant consequences for the growth of destination strategies, policies, and the integration of the information-society dimension. The traditional tourism patterns has undergone a host of changes. Newer rationales for travel and entertainment have led to considerable refinements in this industry that is severely affected by demand considerations. So as the number of tourists swelled, so also a need for newer sites, newer places, experiences and adventures.

**Music tourism** is travel directed towards particular authentic experiences, customized to the interests varying from traditional to contemporary musical interests against the back-drop of culture, arts, ethnic village life, paintings, visiting haunted castles or the like. With the presence of the tourist, money is spent and the local economy benefits. This sort of tourism is particularly important to small villages as well as large cities . Music tourism is one of the newest typologies of tourism and can be categorized under pleasure tourism or special interest tourism . Gibson and Connell , in their widely acclaimed book,"Music and Tourism:on the road again" , deliberately avoid trying to fit 'music tourism' into one neatly-boxed definition. Instead, they take a singularly post-modern view of the topic, demonstrating at the outset that music tourism is a complex social, cultural and economic area of inquiry. Similarly, the authors state that music tourists are also difficult to define. Ultimately, 'music tourism constitutes a cluster of possible tourists, activities, locations, attractions, workers and events which utilise musical resources for tourist purposes' (p. 16).

People are strongly motivated by what a destination has to offer and its relationship to their special interest. Tourism planners and developers in their constant endeavour to give a garb of attractiveness to the intangible tourism offerings, are in recent years concentrating on creating several new tourism themes. A growing number of visitors are becoming special interest travelers who rank music and other art forms, heritage and /or other cultural activities as one of the top five reasons for traveling.

Music plays a central role in virtual tourism, the original means for people to access distant and 'exotic' lands, without ever leaving home. The central tenet is that, by listening to music in everyday life, we are exposed to the 'Other', and this in turn has fuelled our contemporary desire for travel.Music tourism is interwoven around staged events and festivals normally built around an unusual architecture, an engaging piece of history, a curious tradition etc. They instigate valid motives for travel. A musical event can act as a deciding factor by differentiating one destination from another, even resulting in the time change of visits to coincide with the staging of an event, which can be described as 'time switching' factor. In the long run, specific events assist in the development of a destination's image as well as instilling a sense of pride amongst destination communities, both important elements for a tourist destination to cultivate and maintain. Odisha's intriguing staged-events speak of the state's cultural affluence and diversity. Marked by colour and gaiety, these festivals & events are often associated with legends, myths, and even day to day rituals. Every region has its own set of distinctive celebrations that pepper almost all months of the year.

India is a complete world in itself - geographically distinct, a pot-pourri of various cultures, an ancient civilization that has over the years interacted with virtually all the world's races, creeds and ideologies; a land with diverse beliefs, yet preserving the unique flavor which unites the diversity that is India. India from very early days, as early as the Indus period has boasted of a well developed heritage in all forms of art, including architecture, literature, sculpture, painting, music, dance forms, theatre etc. All these were transmitted over generations by word of mouth only, giving rise to communities among clans specializing in a particular discipline The ruling elite patronized and promoted the propagation of arts. Dance and music play a significant role in India as a part of worship, a popular pass-time to woo tourists and as an effective source of entertainment. Among the oldest forms of classical art with a tradition spanning several centuries, the earliest roots of musical forms were embedded in the book "Samaveda".

Since times immemorial, the urge to travel has been spurred by a need. Be it the physicians advice for a change of place or a stress alleviation journey, a pilgrimage to places of religious importance or sight seeing, music has now been interwoven to several tourism campaigns. Music tourism the world over takes a number of forms; as with any other kind of tourism, the commercial end manifests as the kind of mass commodification one sees in Vienna's Mozart chocolate wrappers or Elvis teddybears at Graceland. The other end is the complex set of attractions that draws visitors to particular places in order to listen to the music itself- Salzburg's sing-along Sound of music shows, or Gwalior's music sammelans celebrating the special aspects of the famous Tansen gharana.

Music tourism is a rapidly expanding and diverse tourist niche, although rarely acknowledged by geographers or tourism scholars.There are several significant links between tourism, music and place including museums and festivals, sites of birth and death and (musical) creation, and locations enshrined in lyrics. Of late recognition of the contribution of music tourism to the cultural economy of cities is being emphasized. Music shapes tourist space both aurally and physically, invokes notions of racial and local identity, and contributes to the building of new kinds of economic and cultural networks.

In India there is a steadily growing culture of regional music festivals where the name of the place is becoming increasingly synonymous with the style of music regularly celebrated there by fans on pilgrimage. The deep connection between music and place is the basic premise on which the celebration of classical singing forms like Bhatkhande in

Lucknow and Tyagaraja in Thiruvayyaru in India, or Tamworth for country and Port Fairy for folk in Australia is based. It is the exact opposite of the popular media Song Contests or so-called Idol shows, where – with a few honourable and moving exceptions – cultural differences are flattened out to nothing, and the music is homogenized to fit some synthetic and hypothetical popular-music norm.

Why does a German national get off the plane in Kolkata and head straight to the Star Theatre? This provides a platform for great actors, poets and musicians.An integral part of Bengali history and culture since 1883, it revived itself despite odds and is abuzz with activity again. While the older generation prefers to indulge in nostalgia, the younger generation hang out at the eateries.

Music Tourism grew significantly towards the end of the 20th century, and all forms of music, classical or folk,places of musical composition, places shown on celluloid that became associated with music (as the countryside shown in The Sound of Music) became favourite destinations.The famous "Sound of Music" tours in Salzburg function as a performative space for the construction and narration of Austrian national identity. or those related to a composers place of birth or his death became tourist attractions. Mozart, Bach, Strauss and other classical musicians were crowd pullers and Salzburg became a sort of stage to which tourists flocked. Equally popular was the Vienna Philharmonic Orchestra which played to packed audiences in two big halls, Musikverein and Konzerthaus.

European musical conferences bring together people from far and wide, creating a unique kaleidoscope of colourful cultural patterns. Adelaides Womad festival is an excellent example of tourists and performers who come from the world over to a single destination for music which speaks the language of their land. The program includes the Brazilian singer-songwriter Gilberto Gil, who developed a whole international style dubbed "tropicalismo", incorporating international pop music with South American regional styles and infusing the mix with overt political and social commentary. There's Algerian Hamoud Baroudi, who sang with a German band before going solo and incorporating Algerian, Brazilian and African rhythms and techniques into his work.

The work of other featured artists is more closely tied to a single place, as with the traditional English folk material of Eliza Carthy. Irish band Kila, formed thirteen years ago on the streets of Dublin, shows its Gaelic origins not just in the music but often in the language of the songs. Sultan Khan's music is an unusually pure product of his region and history: he plays traditional classical ragas on the Sarangi, a thirty eight-string Indian violin, of which he's described as an eighth-generation master. Africa, in particular, with its complex and turbulent history, produces artists whose music is intricately tied to the political events of the region. Mali's Oumou Sangare is, through her music, a social commentator and champion for women's rights in Africa, while the Touareg group Tinariwen was formed twenty years ago by young Touareg men in exile. Some of the most intriguing performers are those who have recovered and reclaimed indigenous aspects through music, where original cultures have been destroyed. Oki Kano is a Japanese musician with Ainu (indigenous Japanese) ancestry; he uses the tonkori, a traditional Ainu instrument, to compose new songs with reggae and blues influences as well as to preserve and perform some of the old Ainu songs from Hokkaido. R. Carlos Nakai is a Native American musician and composer, a classically trained trumpet and cornet player whose music for the Native American cedar flute has been award-winning and prolific. Womadelaide takes the place/music connection to a further dimension: a particular city is becoming associated with global diversity. Adelaide is now a place where cultural differences are celebrated annually through the music of the world.

One of the best examples of music tourism is the "Disney Experience", its transition from its early use in cartoons to its current incarnation as a stand-alone product (for example, soundtrack recordings). Charles Carson states, "In the context of Walt Disney World, my belief is that music functions in at least three specific capacities: 1) music links current Disney experiences to (often romanticized) experiences of the past through nostalgia; 2) music defines the boundaries which separate "same" from "other" in terms of both geography and, ultimately, identity; 3) and music serves as an index for the "Disney Experience" in general; an experience which itself is built upon a commixture of the aforementioned modes of identity and nostalgia."

### Fostering Musical Creativity:

Creativity, while highly desirable, is popularly regarded as an elusive, subjective characteristic. Within music, it is reflected largely in compositions. However, creativity can be measured objectively and its involvement of music is not limited to composing. Accumulating findings indicate that musical training enhances intellectual creativity in general.

Mozart is sitting alone in the garden of a country villa on his way from Vienna to Prague. It is September, 1787. Suddenly, the muse "strikes" and immediately he has conceived of the peasant's dance that opens the wedding scene in Act I of, arguably one of the greatest operas ever composed, Don Giovanni. Or so the story goes. Later that day Mozart enthralls the count and countess of the villa, recounting how sitting in the garden had elicited a long-forgotten childhood memory of an afternoon in Italy, and how the two experiences coalesced in his mind to produce the exact music that he needed for the scene. Or so the story goes.

How typical of the creative act. How replete with the romantic vision of artistic insight emanating from a genius for whom creativity was both sublime and effortless. Or so the story goes — for this particular episode is indeed a story, part of an extensive imaginary account of Mozart. It is the creation of Eduard Mörike whose novella, Mozart auf der Reise nach Prag [Mozart on a trip to Prague], published in 1855.

**Music Events of Tourist Importance:**

Indian music (Hindustani in the north and Carnatic in the south) has been evolving as part of India's culture for centuries. Aspects of musical form such as tonal intervals, harmonies and rhythmic patterns are the unique products of a wealth of musical traditions and influences; they are also very different from those familiar in the west. Much of the music recalls Indian fables and legends, as well as celebrating the seasonal rhythms of nature. Indian dancing, similarly unique and timeless, is also widely performed throughout the country, either at major festivals and recitals, or at the many cultural shows which are staged in hotels.

**Music Festivals**
The following is a list of the major music festivals in India:
- Sangeet Natak Akademi - New Delhi.
- January: Tyagaraja - Tiruvayyaru, near Thanjavur.

- March: Shankar Lal – New Delhi.
- August: Vishnu Digambar - New Delhi.
- September: Bhatkhande - Lucknow.
- October: Sadarang - Calcutta.
- November: Sur-Singar - Bombay.
- December: Tansen - Gwalior.
- Music Academy - Madras.
- Shanmukhananda – The Music, Dance, and Drama Festival, Bombay.

## Music Festivals in Odisha:
- **Rajarani Music Festival**

Venue: Rajarani Temple Complex, Bhubaneswar

Rajarani Music Festival is held against the backdrop of the 11th century Rajarani Temple in Bhubaneswar. The city has a large assemblage of celebrated temples of which the Rajarani Temple is one of the most significant. The musical evenings are resplendent with excellent performances by the great maestros of Indian classical music creating an allegory of darbari gayans (musical performances in an Indian king's court) of historical importance. Odisha vis-a-vis India has a great tradition of classical music, instrumental as well as vocal, which fascinate a lot of domestic and international tourists. To show case the glorious tradition of Indian classical music, the Rajarani Music Festival was conceived to be organized by the Department of Tourism in association with organizations like Odisha Sangeet Natak Academy and Bhubaneswar Music Circle.

- **Puri Beach Festival:**

The Puri Beach Festival offers a kaleidoscopic view of Odisha's cultural heritage and modern lifestyle. Spread over five days in the month of November, on the Puri beach, with a backdrop of temples, of which the Lord Jagannath Temple dominates the skyline, it is a showcase of Odisha's reservoir of talent. From cultural events, classical and folk music and dance performances, sand sculptures, handicrafts and food festivals to rock concerts, DJs, beach parties and fashion shows, it has all the ingredients of an international festival.

Indian art, whether it be painting, poetry, dance or music has a characteristically inward quality. This is a manifestation of the bias and world-view of this culture. The nature of creation and its forces are not felt and thought about commencing at the point of material phenomena. Indian thought at its deepest, affirms that mind and matter are rather different grades of the same energy, different organizations of one conscious Force of Existence. Hence the external and its imitation have had little place in our art. The outside is only a projection of this "Force of Existence", experienced within and "beauty does not arise from the subject of a work of art, but from the necessity that has been felt of representing that subject". That is why programmatic music is not considered of really deep quality and it is a recent occurrence in the country, specially with the ballet and the films. Imitations of thunder and the ripple of water is not great music, just as realistic photographic painting is not great art. The languor of rains after an Indian summer is what Malhar expresses but not the patter of drops on a tin roof!

Music, as well as being the most dispensable of arts, is probably the hardest to throw off. Just as memories and landscapes eventually emerge to make emotional claims upon us, music comes uninvited. And stays. It is the lure of place, the call to belong. So the essential purpose of Music would be to dynamically orient the body and mind in relation to the environment, both consciously and unconsciously. Thus the integrated, experiential nature of music makes it a profound and unique way of knowing, being and being well.

*References :*
- Amabile, T. (1983). The Social Psychology of Creativity. New York: Springer-Verlag.
- Ashton, R., (Ed), Music : East and West (Indian Council for Cultural Relations, New Delhi, 1966). A comparative study of Indian and Western Music
- Carson, Charles," Whole New Worlds":Music and the Disney Theme Park experience, in Ethnomusicology Forum, Volume 13, Number 2, November 2004 , pp. 228-235(8)
- Danielou, A., The Ragas of North Indian Music (Munshi Ram Monoharlal Delhi) Notations (staff) of Hindustani ragas.
- Elliot, D. J. (1995). Music Matters. New York: Oxford University Press.
- Goswami, O., The story of Indian Music (Asia, Bombay, 1957). General.
- Rogers, C. (1954). Toward a Theory of Creativity. In Parnes, S. and Harding, H. Eds.), The Sourcebook for Creativity. New York: Scribner.
- Sambamoorthy, P., History of Indian Music (Indian Music Publ. Hs., Madras, 1960). Mainly South Indian.
- Subba Rao, T.V., Studies in Indian Music (Asia, 1965). Collected essays on Karnatak Music.
- Webster, P. (2002). Creative thinking in music: An advanced model. In Sullivan, T. and Williangham, L. (Eds.), Creativity and music education. (pp. 16-34). Toronto: Britannia Printers.

# ISSUES IN INCLUSIVE ORGANISATIONAL DYNAMICS

## Introduction

Over Centuries, India has absorbed supervisory ideas and practices from around the globe. Arlhãshastra codified human resource practices, notions of organisatonal administration, guiding principles and management of personnel (personnel). These are embedded in organisational thinking. Management mindscape continues to be influenced by residual traces of ancient wisdom as it faces complexity of realities. A stream of holistic understanding pervades organisational behaviour at all levels of work. This holds that human nature has a capacity for self-transformation and attaining high ground while facing realities of routine challenges. Such traditions have substantial impact on current organisational mindsets, organisational architecture and organisational practices.

Organisational dynamics is continually changing with organisational complexities, forces of globalisation, accelerated product life cycle, complexity of relationship with stakeholders, scarcity of resources and intense competition. The fate of any organisation largely depends on organisational actions. Increasing 'cut throat' competition and dynamic business environment require a team to run routine operations. Supervisors play a significant role in development, formulation and execution of long term as well as short-term strategies that determine organisational success. Aggregation of personnels' performance represents organisational performance that places stress on efficient use of resources and accomplishment of desirable outcomes. With increased dependency, supervisors are required to sort out ways facilitating organisational expansion. What differentiates surviving organisations is performance and effectiveness of human elements. Reviews reveal three important perspectives;

- Conservative perspectives,
- Organisational level expertise - based perspective, and
- Individual level skill - based perspective.

Studies have traditionally centered upon practice and arrangement that produce social or civilizing distinctions that underlie prohibiting and societal disparity. Their endeavour has been to understand how and when in times gone by of modern social order those distinctions were shaped, why they mattered for cohort of institutions, such as organization building and restructuring. Furthermore, research has focused on ways social division have entered into organizational decision-making, how new categories of distinction have come out to become sources of inequity and what could be done to contest direct and indirect forms of discrimination in organizations. In this regard, much valuable understanding has added to understanding of exclusionary mechanisms on level of social interaction, group processes and organizational policy. However, with this focal point on organizational exclusion, a condition for inclusion and idea of inclusiveness tend to be disregarded. The objective, in this paper, is to bring out new points of view and gain fresh thoughts by thought-provoking reflection upon inclusion and inclusiveness. Catchphrase of 'inclusive organization' has been circulating in practice and diversity teaching. It occurs in condition of managing change through visualizing goals of change. Management and personnels are upbeat to consider their organization, place of work, team - processes, etc., in terms of inclusiveness, focus upon benefits of change, positive impact on cooperation, organizational background and individual well-being. 'Making of inclusion' needs to be regarded as combined effort by various change agents, in positioned framework. In terms of tactic, multi-level scrutiny allows for investigations of distinctiveness. This argues for a need to conceive inclusive organization from theory-based perspective to interdisciplinary field of multiplicity investigation. There is a need to address, How to forecast inclusive organizations? How to visualize processes and mechanisms of inclusion? Which models of inclusion are apt to highlight dynamics of 'making of inclusion'? How to conceive link between inclusion and diversity? How to conceive relationship between inclusiveness and equal opportunity? How can models add to understanding of inclusive organizations? How do institutional environments contribute to inclusiveness? How to conceive inclusive organizations on group-dynamics?

## Conceptualisation

'Culture' is something that an organisation has. Culture adds to organisation as a whole. Culture can be manipulated and altered. Inclusive organisational culture is a pattern of shared basic assumptions invented, discovered, or developed as it learns to cope with its problems of external adaptation and internal integration that have worked well enough to be considered valid. It is defined as 'specific collection of values and norms that are shared by personnel and groups in an organisation and that control the way they interact with and outside the organisation.' Inclusive organisational culture is a set of shared mental assumptions that guide interpretation and action by defining appropriate behavior.

'Conservative 'approaches' have been inadequate. They have been based on outmoded models of organisational dynamics. Complexity approaches offer a new perspective, or paradigm, which leads to a radically different kind of practice for agents. Notion of culture lead us to think of culture as a 'thing' or a state which 'belongs' to an organisation. This is in those models that distinguish different 'types' of organisational culture. This conventional approach is summarised as:

- Where do we need to be going strategically as an organisation?
- Where are we now as a culture?
- What are the gaps between where we are as a culture and where we should be?
- What is our sketch of action to seal those gaps?

The paradigm is what the organisation is about. What it does? Whata are its mission and its values. Two main reasons why inclusive cultures develop in organizations is due to external adaptation and internal integration. External adaptation reflects evolutionary approach to inclusive organizational inclusive culture and suggests that inclusive cultures develop and persist because they organization to survive and flourish. If inclusive culture is valuable, then it holds potential for generating sustained competitive advantages. Additionally, internal integration is an important function since structures are required for organizations to exist. Inclusive practices are learnt through socialization at workplace. Work environments reinforce inclusive culture on daily basis by encouraging personnels to exercise cultural values.

'Emergence' is a key attribute. It is unexplained and ordinary. Patterns or global-level structures arise from interactive local-level processes by the process. This 'pattern' cannot be understood or predicted from behavior or properties of component units alone. Most change is emergent. It comes about because of interactions between 'agents' in system. In an organisation the agents are personnel; themselves complex systems. Complexity suggests that when there is enough connectivity between agents emergence, is likely to occur instinctively. Four general dimensions; Mission (Strategic Direction and Intent, Goals and Objectives and Vision), Adaptability (Creating Change, Customer Focus and Inclusive organisational Learning), Involvement (Empowerment, Team Orientation and Capability Development) and Consistency (Core Values, Agreement, Coordination/Integration) describe inclusive organisational culture.

Some parameters in inclusive analyses include;
- Control Systems: The processes in place to monitor what is going on. Role cultures would have vast rulebooks. There would be more reliance on individualism in a power culture.
- Inclusive organisational Structures: Reporting lines, hierarchies, and the way that work flows through the business.
- Power Structures: Who makes the decisions, how widely spread is power and on what is power based?

- Symbols: These include inclusive organisational logos and designs, but also extend to symbols of power such as parking spaces and executive washrooms.
- Rituals and Routines: Management meetings, board reports and so on may become more habitual than necessary.

Inclusive organisational culture is shaped by multiple factors:

- External environment,
- Industry/ Technology,
- Size and nature of organisation 's workforce,
- Organisation's history and ownership,
- Acceptance and appreciation for diversity,
- Regard for and fair treatment of personnel,
- Respect for each personnel's contribution,
- Personnel pride and enthusiasm for organization and work performed,
- Equal opportunity for personnel to realize potential,
- Strong communication,
- Strong organisation leaders,
- Strong sense of direction and purpose,
- Ability to compete,
- Lower than average turnover rates, and
- Investment in learning, training, and personnel knowledge.

An inclusive culture involves full and successful integration of diverse personnel into a workplace or industry. While an inclusive culture certainly encompasses a commitment to workplace diversity, it is not limited simply to basic representation; it indicates a climate in which respect, equity, and positive recognition of differences are all cultivated, and the social and institutional response to disability poses no barrier to a positive employment

experience. Additionally, inclusive cultures extend beyond basic or token presence of personnels who have disabilities. They encompass both formal and informal policies and practices, and involve several core values:
- Representation: Presence of personnel with a range of personnel roles and leadership positions.
- Receptivity: Respect for differences in working styles and flexibility.
- Fairness: Equitable access to all resources, opportunities, networks and decision-making processes.

### Inclusive organizational and Disorder Complexity

What failings in inclusive model are claimed to be corrected? How novel are prescriptions derived from complexity model? How plausible? Does complexity model provide scientific back up? This is complexity model (within which 'disorder' is a mode of behaviour) concerned with behaviour over time of certain kinds of complex systems. Aspects of this become focus of attention. The systems of interest to complexity model, under certain conditions, perform in regular, predictable ways; under other conditions, they exhibit behaviour in which regularity and predictability is lost. Almost imperceptible differences in preliminary conditions guide to steadily diverging system reactions until finally evolution of behaviour is dissimilar.

Justifications start from description of pre-existing state of inclusive organizational model and practice, which stresses its unacknowledged but self-imposed limitations and tunnel vision. These subsequently transcend complexity-based philosophy. Agreed that key finding is effective unknowability of future, assumption is to decide where inclusive organizational is going and take decisions designed to get it there is hazardous. Inclusive organizational, afflicted by increasing complexity react by becoming quite intolerant of ambiguity. Factors, targets, structures need to be nailed. Uncertainty is ignored or denied. Inclusive task is enunciation of mission, determination of strategy and elimination of deviation. Stability is sought as ultimate fortification against anxiety, which otherwise become overwhelming. All these reflexes, are counter-productive when viewed from complexity point of view.

The above explanation convergences into;
- Inclusive organizations adapt to their environments and help them,
- Success comes from contradiction as well as consistency,
- Success may stem from being part of a self-reinforcing cycle, rather than from an explicit vision, and
- Revolutionary as well as incremental changes lie on route to inclusive organizationa success.

Could inclusive organizational complexity deprived of scientific authority claim that results from complexity model hold for inclusive organization by equivalence? The requirements would require;
- Scientific domain of complexity model is better understood ,
- Causal connection between groups of concepts is implicitly preserved between equivalents.
- Whether Complexity model is established in field of inclusive dynamics.
- What inclusive aspects are to be positioned in complexity model.

**Discussion**

As inclusion becomes the focus of diversity work, the attention switches to the systems, policies and practices of

the organisation. Do personnels in all groups and categories feel comfortable and welcomed in the inclusive organizational? Do they feel included and do they experience the environment as inclusive? In the last few years, focus has shifted from diversity to inclusion. In most organizations, inclusion has been added with no explanation. Several systems influence inclusiveness:
- Communications
- Work assignment
- Training and education
- Performance management
- Mentoring
- Coaching
- Hiring
- Career development
- Flexible work arrangements
- Supervisors' accountability

**FIGURE 1**
**PHASES OF ORGANISATIONAL INCLUSIVE DYNAMICS**

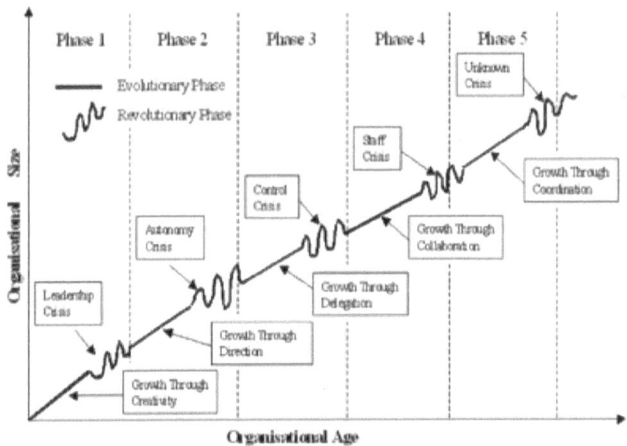

Greiner's model, above, suggests how organisations grow, but basic reasons behind inclusive dynamics process and its mechanics remain unclear. As mentioned previously, inclusive dynamics in a living organisation is a result of the interplay between ontogenic factor and environment. Here, positive feedback plays a vital role. Although both positive and negative feedback work, in order to grow (or to effect other changes in a system), net type of feedback must be positive. This means that more they grow, more capacity in resources acquisition they have and more resources they can access. This inclusive dynamics and increase in resource acquisition capabilities provide a positive feedback loop, which continues until organisation matures. Positive feedback loop will be active again when organisation starts to decline, which will be mentioned later.

Organisation cannot perpetually maintain inclusive dynamics, nor can it ensure its survival and viability forever. After its inclusive dynamics, system matures declines and eventually ends. This can be explained by using concept of 'homeokinesis'. Homeostasis is described in homeokinetic terms as a 'homeokinetic plateau'. Although it is argued that, the concept and net positive feedback can be applied to explanation of deterioration and demise in organisations. It is difficult to make a direct homology between changes in organisations and changes in organisations. Rather than being biological machines, which can be described and explained, to a large extent if not (arguably) completely, organisations are much more complex socio-technical systems comprising ensembles of personnel, artefacts, and technology working together in an organised manner.

## FIGURE 2
## BOUNDS OF HOMOKINETIC PLATEAU

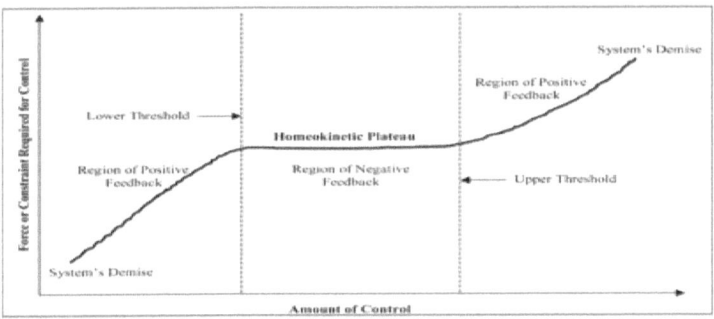

Degree of systemic change depends on magnitude of environmental contingencies or external fluctuations although internal fluctuations play vital role in inducing change in complex systems. Based on argument made, organisation as a complex system can neither always maintain itself in a steady state (or homeostasis) nor keep on transforming without reference to the magnitude of fluctuations or disturbances that impinge upon it. It is difficult for major transformational change to occur, or be implemented, because it typically involves profound reformulation of organisation's mission, structure, management and fundamental changes in inclusive aspects. Hence, this covers both operational processes and psychological dimensions of organisations. Transformational change requires energy (both human and non-human) to push organisation across instability threshold by means of necessary fluctuations, from within and without, to inflict morphological change. Organisations as systems can only maintain their steady state or remain in a homeostatic equilibrium.

**Strategy**

Organisations as complex systems can be manipulated by using 'Management Systems Model' or MSM. The systemic tools or factors, available to manage or manipulate organisations in a desired way are:

- Strategy
- Structure
- Procedures (technology/process)
- Culture
- Leadership

This model implies that each systemic tool should be applied in a harmonised and thoughtful manner to yield best possible result as each particular tool or factor, when applied, would yield a different systemic result. While leadership and strategy are generally tools for inflicting changes or destabilisation on organisations, culture, procedures or technology and structure are systemic tools that are typically used to impose stability and regulation in the organisation. Moreover, dynamic behaviour of organisation is a result of interplay between these endogenous factors and environment and interaction among these endogenous factors themselves (interaction among strategy, leadership, structure, procedures and culture). Rather than being considered as manipulating tools, each factor can be treated as organisational property that can be changed to suit both external and internal contingencies. However, effort required to change each property varies. Transformation requires a tremendous amount of energy, in terms of resources and effort, to change organisational culture and the political network as well.

## FIGURE 3
## INTERFACE FOR INCLUSIVE CHANGE

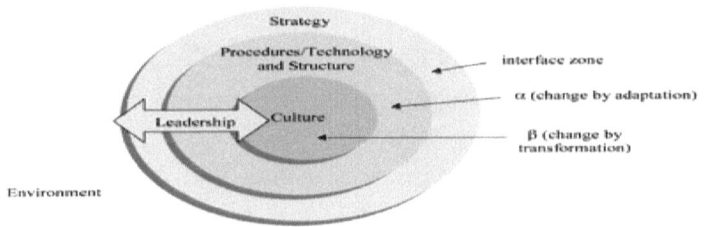

In order for an organisation to operate successfully in a specific environment, it needs an interface between its subsystems and the environment. Organisational strategy is such an interface. The next layer is the zone in which interplay between technology, process and structure to carry out organisation's operations exists and is active. Variables and factors in this zone are more sensitive to disturbance from both internal and external sources and less difficult to manage and change than those from the inner core. This ensemble of variables can be changed, with a certain effort, to achieve a proper alignment with the environment called adaptation. The impact of culture on organisations is pervasive because it controls personnel's beliefs and shared values, and it is transferable from one generation to next. It is thus unlikely that culture can easily be changed or adjusted to conform to changing environment. It requires a great deal of energy, effort and time to change existing culture and this is beyond adaptive mechanism. That is called cultural level deep change.

In adaptation, changes in environment require that organisations modify some of their properties (strategy, structure, procedures or technology, and size) to be aligned with that environment. However, adaptation cannot accommodate cultural change, which involves changing of personnel's beliefs held at a deep level. When organisations have to cope with an extremely high environmental contingency, transformation, which is a more substantial and pervasive form of change that includes the change of organisational culture and its political web, must be introduced to ensure their survival. Since environment of organisations is ever more complex and dynamic, it is argued that a unified model, which encompasses both adaptation and transformation, should be developed and empirically tested with the aim of better representing and understanding change in organisations.

*Lt Col J Satpathy and Prof Adyasha Das*

### References

- Bak, P. (1997) How Nature Works: The Science of Self-Organized Criticality. Oxford: University Press, USA.
- Capra, F.(1997) The Web of Life: A New Synthesis of Mind and Matter. London: Flamingo, UK.
- Dooley, K. J. and Van de Ven, A. H. (1999) 'Explaining Complex Organizational Dynamics' Organization Science Vol. 10, No. 3 May-June pp. 358-372, USA.
- Douglas, M. (1985) 'Introduction' in Jonathan L. Gross and Steve Rayner, Measuring Culture: A Paradigm for the Analysis of Social Organization. New York: Columbia University Press, USA.
- Geertz, C. (1973) The Interpretation of Culture. New York: Basic Books, USA.
- Handy, C. (1995) Gods of Management: The Changing
Work of Organisations. London: Arrow, UK.

- Harrison, R. and Stokes, H. (1992) Diagnosing Organizational Culture. San Francisco: Pfeiffer, USA.
- Johnson, G. (1992) 'Managing Strategic Change — Strategy, Culture and Action'. Long Range Planning Vol 25 No 1 pp 28-36, USA.
- Kauffmann, S.A. (1993) The Origins of Order: self-organisation and selection in evolution, Oxford University Press, New York, USA.
- Kroeber, A.L. and Kluckhohn, C. (1952) 'Culture: A Critical Review of Concepts and Definitions.' Papers of the Peabody Museum of Harvard Achæology and Ethnology, Harvard University 42(1). Cambridge, Mass: Museum Press, USA.
- Kuhn, T. (1996) The Structure of Scientific Revolutions. 3rd ed. Chicago: University Press, USA.
- Merry, U. (1995) Coping With Uncertainty: insights from the new sciences of disorder, self-organisation and complexity, Praeger, Westport, Conn, USA.
- Mihata, K. (1997) 'The Persistence of 'Emergence" in Raymond A. Eve, Sara Horsfall and Mary E. Lee (eds) Chaos, Complexity and Sociology: Myths, Models and Theories pp 30-38. Thousand Oaks, Ca: Sage, USA.
- Mitleton-Kelly E. (1997) 'Organisations as co-evolving complex adaptive systems'. BPRC Paper No.5, Business Process Resource Centre, University of Warwick, Coventry, UK.
- Morgan, G. (1997) Images of Organization. 2nd ed. Thousand Oaks: Sage, USA.
- Phillips, L. (1993) 'Facilitated work groups: model and practice', J. Opl Res. Soc. 44 (pp 533-549), USA.
- Rosenhead, J. (ed.)(1989a) Rational Analysis for a Problematic World: problem structuring methods for

- complexity, uncertainty and conflict, Wiley, Chichester, UK.
- Shallice, T. (1996) 'The domain of supervisory processes and temporal organisation of behaviour', Phil. Trans. Roy. Soc. Lond., 351 (pp 1405-1412) , UK.
- Shaw, P. (1997) 'Intervening in the Shadow Systems of Organizations: Consulting from a Complexity Perspective.' Journal of Organizational Change Management **10**(3): 235-250, USA.
- Sperber, D. 1996. Explaining Culture: A Naturalistic Approach. Oxford: Blackwell, UK.
- Stacey, R. D. (1992) Managing The Unknowable: strategic boundaries between order and disorder in organisations, Jossey-Bass, San Francisco, USA.
- ——————— (1993) Strategic Organisation and Organisational Dynamics, Pitman, London, UK.
- ——————— (1996) Complexity and Creativity in Organisations, Berrett-Koehler, San Fransisco, USA.
- Wheatley, M. J. (1992) Leadership and the New Science: learning about organisation from an orderly universe, Berrett-Koehler, San Francisco, USA.
- Wilkins, A. L. and Patterson, K. J. (1985) 'You Can't Get There From Here: What Will Make Culture-Change Projects Fail'. in R. H. Kilmann, M. J. Saxton, R. Serpa and associates (eds) Gaining Control of the Organisational Culture. San Francisco: Jossey-Bass, 262-291, USA.

# SUFISM AS A WAY OF LIFE

> *"There are two aspects of individual harmony: the harmony between body and soul, and the harmony between individuals. All the tragedy in the world, in the individual and in the multitude, comes from lack of harmony. And harmony is best given by producing harmony in one's own life."*
> *- Hazrat Inayat Khan*

In the past few years, Sufism has reached unprecedented heights of popularity the world over. The current and growing interest in Sufism can be understood by focussing on the same factors which account for the popularity of several diverse Eastern mystical traditions among Westerners. These include a craving for life-transforming spiritual experiences, and an attraction to monistic belief systems. British orientalist Martin Lings commented: "A Vendantist, a Taoist, or a Buddhist can find in many aspects of Islamic mysticism, a 'home from home,' such as he could less easily find in Christianity or Judaism."' In a world torn apart by strife and turbulence, stress has overwhelmed the life of the individual. This article presents Sufism as a model for helping to alleviate human miseries, a transcendence from the individual to a spiritual height. As the instability, contradictions, and stress of the socioeconomic structure create a frantic search for relevant modes of treatment, the Sufi theories present an alternative approach to be taken up in the interest of more effective practice. Sufism and its principles appear to be the ideal way of life in contemporary conditions. The Sufi Way is a mystical order dedicated to awakening of one's inner self and forging friendly ties with one and all. By "awakening" we refer to direct recognition of pure awareness, the nameless unity of Being. By "friendship" we mean a warm-hearted embrace toward all — ourselves, our loved ones, our world, and all creation.

Sufi teachings and practices are an amalgamation drawn from all traditions in a spirit of respect and creativity. Sufism has profoundly influenced such notable founders of new religious movements as George I. Gurdjieff and Bhagwan Shree Rajneesh. Also, several personalities who have made their mark outside of the field of religion acknowledge the influence of Sufism on their lives, including novelist Doris Lessing, actor James Coburn, poets Ted Hughes and Robert Graves, psychologists Erich From and Robert Ornstein, and the late Secretary-General of the United Nations Dag Hammarskjold.

**A celebration of life with Discipline, Piety and Mysticism**

Sufis have endeavoured to make a science of the subjective. They have developed perhaps the most systematic and monitored progression into the mystical there is. For a serious seeker of mystical experience this aspect is most attractive, for it conveys the impression of a venerable tradition that can be trusted to impart authentic spiritual knowledge.

The Sufi way of life is very much concerned with

perfecting of the individual disciple. This endeavour is known as *work* . The work is prescribed by the Shaikh, performed by the Sufi, in the context of the community. It aims to break the hold of conditioned patterns of behaviour which inhibit the desired spiritual awakening.

Most Sufi orders consider the first work of the disciple to be the observance of traditional Islamic piety: to perform the "five pillars." The Sufis' exceptional spiritual hunger, however, will urge them to go far beyond the stipulated observations. For example, in addition to observing the nightly fasts required during the month of Ramadan, Sufis frequently engage in voluntary fasts.

The use of dance for spiritual purposes has become one of the most defining characteristics of Sufism, though not all of the orders observe it. According to Martin Lings, many Sufis have the conviction that "the body stands for the Axis of the Universe which is none other than the Tree of Life. The dance is thus a rite of centralisation, intended above all to plunge the dancer into a state of concentration upon Allah."

Meditation is an essential part of the Sufi's work at self-perfection. Repetition of a *dhikr* or sacred formula (e.g., the name of Allah) is often combined with breathing exercises to induce altered states of consciousness.

"As the natural mental barriers to psychic intrusion are broken down, and a link is established to the spirit world, the Sufi may see visions, hear the voices of angels and prophets, and gain from them guidance. It is a condition of joy and longing. And when this condition seizes on the "seeker," he falls into ecstasy. The dervishes in the monasteries may be seen working themselves up into a condition of "ecstasy."

Such spectacles will not be viewed in the same

favourable light by all observers. John Alden Williams points out that the observer may encounter things which seem to belong in a case book of abnormal psychology, or witness what looks remarkably like demonic possession. But unless he is wholly unsympathetic, he may find also in these sweating ecstatics examples of pure and devoted attendance upon the Holy.

## SUFISM IN THE MODERN ERA

By the eighteenth and nineteenth centuries Islam had accumulated an amazing diversity of religious ideas and customs; the acceptance of Sufism into the orthodox fold had no small part to play in this discoloration of the faith. To the bulk of humanity the call to abjure the world and to dedicate ourselves to complete absorption in the contemplation of the Divinity is an inducement to mental lethargy. The quietism of the Sufi Mystical teachings like the following may be noted: the man who looks on the beggar's bowl as a kingly crown And the present world as a fleeting bubble He alone traverseth the ocean of Truth Who looks upon life as a fairy talecan have but one result–intellectual paralysis.However, "for the last forty years the direct and indirect influence of the East has prepared the ground in the West for the seed of the Sufi message."

### Sufism and the path of the heart:

In Sufi terminology, "heart" signifies the biological heart's spiritual aspect as the centre of all emotions and (intellectual and spiritual) faculties, such as perception, consciousness, sensation, reasoning, and willpower. Sufis call it the "human truth"; philosophers call it the "speaking selfhood" (Gülen, 2006, p. 22).

In describing Islam, some Muslim scholars use the

analogy of a walnut. The practical, ritual and legal dimensions of the Islamic faith are likened to the outer shell. Inside this shell one finds the animating spiritual core, also known as the Sufi path, which is signified by the inner kernel. The oil that permeates all parts of the walnut represents the all-encompassing nature of Ultimate Reality, or God.

In the same manner that the shell provides protection to the kernel, the legal and obligatory rituals provide the form within which the spiritual life is allowed to ripen. Simultaneously, the kernel gives life to the shell without which it would be an empty form, barren and purposeless. The driving force of creation and human life is divine love and mercy. The Sufi longs for an intimate experience of the divine presence that brings him into direct contact with his true and most fundamental nature.

Sufi devotion has not only been reflected in sublime love poetry, music and dance, but also in rigorous spiritual practices that overcome all that veils the lover from the Beloved. In diligently following the various techniques of self-cultivation, the seeker "polishes the mirror of the heart". The human heart in the Islamic tradition is the most encompassing abode of the divine. Passing through a number of stages, often guided by a spiritual teacher, the seeker's spiritual evolution ideally culminates in a state of being in which there is a collapse of boundaries between the seeker and the Sought. Here the Sufi holds sacrosanct God's promise: "My servant continues to draw near me through free acts of devotion until I love him. When I love him, I am the eye with which he sees, the hearing with which he hears, the tongue with which he speaks and the hand with which he grasps."

To enable refinement of the character, the Sufi is

encouraged to cultivate social interactions based on, qualities of love, mercy, justice, compassion, generosity and gentleness.

The goal of a Sufi is "to love every life as your own". Thus, spiritual development demands an ethics of care that is socially engaged.

Taming, mastering and purifying the various inclinations of the lower self is not simply an individualistic spirituality but also one that intrinsically breaks down barriers between self and "other", thus demanding a spiritually-imbued communal ethics.

In fact, the central love motif of early Sufism dates back to the most famous eighth-century woman Sufi, Rabia Al-Adawiyya. Rabia is seen as the model mystic who ran down the streets of the Basra of present-day Iraq carrying a torch in one hand and a bucket of water in the other, saying that she wanted to set fire to Heaven and extinguish the flames of Hell, so that the seekers of God could rip down the veils of distraction, and so focus on the true goal that was the Divine Beloved. When Sufism reflects radical forms of gender equality, this is because gender is considered irrelevant to the ultimate goal of the mystical path, which makes equal demands on men and women.

In Sufi writings, there are extra-ordinary narratives of love and sexuality between human beings. In the 15th century Abd al-Rahman Jami reflects on the spiritual and pedagogic value of human love as a ladder by which humans ascend to an experience of divine love. The 13th century Andalusian Sufi mystic Muhyideen Ibn Arabi states more radically that sexual union provides the Sufi with a taste of mystical annihilation and is a locus for the disclosure of the divine.

These Sufi imaginations of gender highlight the

spiritual value of love relationships and create expansive possibilities for re-thinking gender ethics in Muslim societies.

In reality, of course, one finds all shades of Sufi aspirants. There are those who embody beautiful character, and diligently strive to embody the divine attributes, those who are socially engaged, those who withdraw from society, those who are gender egalitarian, those who are sexist, those whose socio-political engagements emerge from their commitment to Sufi virtues, those who use Sufism for particular vested socio-political interests, and those who are charlatans.

Ultimately, however, the criterion for distinguishing a true Sufi must be sought in the normative standards of the Sufi paradigm. Here the simple yet profound tradition of the Prophet Muhammad is most insightful: "Among the best of you is the one most beautiful in character."

### Divine Forgiveness:

*Duality vanished, I become You, and you I. Your love does not empty while my ego is tamed. I stuck in my foot, halting union with You O King, Master, Lover. Walking your path is my life's only comfort. Romance is only a bridge to Your love. Humans have the same soul, but our bodies are millions. Many languages there are, but they all mean the same. Our minds and heads one, reality's essence is one also. Liberation from selfishness, reconciliation is kindness.*

### The Divine Forgiveness Cluster

*– a way to address layers of self-isolation and disconnection*

The subject of forgiveness, and what forgiveness means to human beings, immediately brings up the issue of the sense of self-worth. By examining the cluster of divine

Names that comprise the forgiveness family, we have a unique opportunity to address crippling human problems such as self-loathing, guilt, and shame. The four Names in the forgiveness family offer an excellent way to describe and understand the different gradations of Divine Forgiveness and provide an effective avenue for spiritual growth.

The ground floor in the forgiveness cluster of Names, the starting point, is al-Ghaffar. It is appropriate to begin with this divine quality as it relates to a low point in the human process. People at this stage are usually unable to even consider the possibility of forgiveness. They are caught up in disbelief, grief, and judgment—often self-judgment. There is a progression of forgiveness implied in the Qur'an. *Do the big forgiveness, and if you can't do that, do a lesser forgiveness, and if you can't do that, do a still lesser* forgiveness.

There is a focus on applying the healing properties of the forgiveness family to the human condition, and in particular to our emotional and mental health.

There is a memorable hadith where a Bedouin says to the Prophet, "What if I do this really bad thing?" And the answer is, "Allah forgives." "But what if I do it again and again and again?" "Allah continues to forgive." Then the Bedouin says, "Doesn't Allah ever get tired of forgiving?" And the Prophet Muhammad says, "No, but you might get tired of doing that same thing over and over again."

Al-Ghafur goes right to the worst crime we have ever committed in our lives. It goes right to the worst thing that has ever been done to us. Whether it is a grudge of self-loathing or a grudge held against another, the depth of feeling is the same. Allah's forgiveness reaches that deepest place. From a medical point of view we might say that al-

Ghaffar is a remedy for a chronic condition and Al-Ghafur is for an acute condition.

The very concept of forgiveness, even in English usage, is to give up the grudge, to let go of that revenge fantasy. Forgiveness comes by giving that away. So at this first stage in the process of learning to forgive, one needs to learn to give up the revenging impulse that arises many times a day. And one also needs to give up the grudge one may hold about the inner wound perceived to be unforgiveable.

Going beyond this, there is an inner stage called tawba. Now one is actually able to turn away from perceived defects and shadows and face directly towards the divine perfection. At-Tawwab is both the divine reality that one turns to in such a way and the activity of turning. The form in Arabic is wa taaba ilallaah. We literally turn from the defect and toward Allah. "From" and "toward" are expressed simultaneously by the same verb in Arabic.

The ultimate stage of forgiveness is expressed by al-'Afuw. Imagine an image of the wind blowing across the desert vastness and completely erasing all the tracks in the sand. It is as if no one had ever walked there. Such a fundamental image in the root of the word shows us that with al-'Afuw, one does not even notice the fault.

In the first stages of forgiveness the fault is easily noticed, but there is a possibility for forgiveness, a chance for some healing salve to reach the wounded places. Then one finds the strength to overlook it. Eventually it becomes possible to turn away from the fault towards Allah whenever awareness of the fault arises, thus transforming negativity into a vision of the divine face.

Finally we come to al-'Afuw, which means to completely forgive, with no trace of the fault even subtly retained. There is not even a trace of resentment or memory.

There are no footprints in the sand. There are no impressions. Your awareness is clean and incapable of being stained. Such is the highest stage of divine forgiveness.

## Good Neighbourliness and Sufism

*"We must not imagine that such global issues as peace and justice can be undertaken, or even addressed in a meaningful way, by any one religious tradition alone. For we are not alone in this world. We share our world with people of all cultures, races, and religions, and our future is one"* (p.8)

Cited in Diana L. Eck: "A perspective in Dialogue: Looking ahead" in Current Dialogue-8 June 1985.

There is the need to firmly recognize the Inter-relatedness and inter-dependence of the human family.Since in Islam, the means to an end is often as crucial as the end itself we must work within a process which is in accordance with the end we seek to achieve/ attain.

Hence, understanding the other is very crucial. We need to understand the other but even more than that we need each other. It is when we look closely into the eyes of our neighbour that we see ourselves and understand ourselves better.There must be a shared consciousness of God's will and way.

This should create mutual spiritual enlightenment/ upliftment. Our relationship with people of other faiths must be founded on mutual speaking and listening, giving and taking/sharing, agreeing and disagreeing .

### *Sufism: a celebration of life*

Sufi poetry, music and dance have long been used for mental health intervention in order to heal and cure people who are experiencing anxiety, depression and stress (Mirdal, 2012, p. 1008). Poems or songs talking about the pleasures of drinking bitter red wine and intoxication, or spending a long dark night of passion with a beautiful one are quite common in Sufi literature. This was a wish-fulfilment for many while leading to a poetic/musical healing.

The origin of stress, according to Sufism, is the restlessness of the human soul. To remedy a problem effectively one has to ascertain its root. According to the Sufic model, the Creator has predetermined everything that happens. One of the primary aims of Sufism is to train the body, soul and mind not to complain about life (Nazim, 2002). When we stop complaining, life becomes calm, and stressful life events are bearable. This is the greatest merit of the Sufic model. However, this does not mean that we do not have to do anything to alleviate stress should it occur. This is when the intervention of zikirullah is therapeutic. The merit of zikirullah is that through it we develop the capacity to discriminate internal stimuli, such as stress, memories, fears, anger and depression, as it provides measures of enhancing our self-awareness, which is useful in empathizing, relating and communicating our responses in social situations.

A common-sensical understanding of Sufism has led to a number of products being sold as stress-alleviation strategies.

**Two cases:**
**Jashn-e-Sufi**

*Sufiyana Celebration of Ishq..Ibadat..Zikr..* Knocking has ceased. The moment is ripe. The door, opens. The path is drunken. Method, celebration. This monsoon, we have invited Nirupam and Damini for a unique Sufi jugalbandi at Zorba. A special three day Sufiyana Intensive. Combining the dynamics of tradition and with contemporary techniques. Sufi qaul from South Asia flowing with the techniques of Zikr from the Middle East. The feminine and masculine aspects of the path, meeting, merging. The techniques of Ibadat, meet the fragrance of Ishq. Creating the Sama, the state of ecstatic union.

*What to expect* : Nirupam will be leading you into the depths of remembrance through Zikr and a special session of Sufi healing. Damini will be guiding you into the heights of ecstasy through Sama, a cocktail of handpicked Sufi stories, music and mystical sounds. And, of course, there will be Sufiyana dancing, plus. They have designed the intensive to include contemporary Sufi methods from the world of Osho. There will be an initiation into techniques that can be carried back home.

*What is the motive* : An invitation into the Sufi esoteric path in a simple, easy, contemporary manner. With techniques that can be practised in your daily life. For - as the wise Sufis have said - only a desperation of thirst, combined with a sincerity of practise, can make that moment arrive ... when the door, opens. And the real celebration, Jashn-e-Sufi, begins.

Guests of numerous religious and ethnic backgrounds converged on Wheeler Auditorium to listen to music, meditate and learn lessons about Sufism, a movement that preaches a path to self-knowledge.

UC Berkeley's MTO Sufi Association held the campus's third annual Sufi Celebration—called "The Hidden Angles of Life," to educate students and community members about the philosophy, first taught 1,400 years ago. Sufism preaches that a harmonious society can only be achieved when all of its members attain self-cognition.

As a result, the teachings appeal to people from a wide array of religious and ethnic backgrounds, said senior Negar Dadgari, an architecture major and president of the association. "Our goal is to raise spiritual awareness on campus and to just really expand love and unity," Dadgari said.

After opening remarks about the movement, musicians played modern instruments and sang in harmony with the traditional santur, setar and daf. "Teachers of Sufism have always taught to a broad and diverse group of students," Dadgari said in opening remarks.

The celebration concluded with a speech on tamarkoz, the ability to achieve bodily self-awareness, followed by a demonstration of movazeneh, or meditation. The audience was then led in guided meditation. "Sufism is essentially a path to self-knowledge," said Sahar Yousef, freshman cognitive science and philosophy major. "Once you're on this path it's like you're wooing the god within you."

The current master of the School of Islamic Sufism is Nader Angha, who lives in Germany and broadcasts weekly, live webcasts for Sufis to study, Dadgari said.

Sufism is essentially a way of life, a celebration called life.It is best understood as that by most lay men. Stephen Prothero in his book "God is not one" writes:

*Mystics often claim that the great religions differ only in the inessentials. They may be different paths but they are ascending the same mountain and they converge at the peak. Throughout this book I give voice to these mystics: the Daoist sage Laozi, who wrote his classic the Daodejing just before disappearing forever into the mountains; the Sufi poet Rumi, who instructs us to "gamble everything for love"; and the Christian mystic Julian of Norwich, who revels in the feminine aspects of God. But my focus is not on these spiritual superstars. It is on ordinary religious folk—the stories they tell, the doctrines they affirm, and the rituals they practice. And these stories, doctrines, and rituals could not be more different. Christians do not go on the hajj to Mecca; Jews do not affirm the doctrine of the Trinity; and neither Buddhists nor Hindus trouble themselves about sin or salvation.*

In conclusion to quote one of the most ardent Sufi practitioners, *"'....Our work for peace must begin within the private world of each one of us. To build for man a world without fear, we must be without fear. To build a world of justice, we must be just. And how can we fight for liberty if we are not free in our own minds? How can we ask others to sacrifice if we are not ready to do so?... Only in true surrender to the interest of all can we reach that strength and independence, that unity of purpose, that equity of judgment which are necessary if we are to measure up to our duty to the future, as men of a generation to whom the chance was given to build in time a world of peace.'"* (UN Press Release SG/360, December 22, 1953)

Dag Hammerskjold, Sufi

Late Secretary General of United Nations

The year he died, he was awarded the Nobel Peace Prize posthumously. (Today, the United Nations dedicates an entire region of their website to Hammarskjöld.)

**References:**
Arasteh, S. R. (1965). *Rumi The Persian: Rebirth in creativity and love.* Lahore: Pakistan.
Chittick, W. (2008). *Sufism. A Beginner's Guide.* Oxford, U.K.: One World.
Frager, Robert, *Heart, Self & Soul: The Sufi Psychology of Growth, Balance, and Harmony*
Fromm, E. (1956). *The art of loving.* NY: Harper & Brothers Publishers.
Hammerskjold, Dag(2006)."*Markings*": Vintage Haque, Amber (2004), "*Psychology from Islamic*
*Perspective: Contributions of Early Muslim Scholars and Challenges to Contemporary Muslim Psychologists*", *Journal of Religion and Health*
Memon, Q. B. & Zeeshan Yousaf, Z. (2013). "*I am a poet of Workers and peasants.*" *World Literature,* 87(6), 47-50.
Nizamie, S. H., Katshu, M. Z. U. H. & Uvais, N. A. (2013). Sufism and mental health. *Indian Journal of Psychiatry,* 55, S215-S223.

# FROM SELF TO SELF: SUFISM AND TRANSCULTURAL EXPRESSIONS

Sufism embodies as an idea, imagery, literary knowledge, critical heritage, discourse and practice in Muslim societies and Indian/South Asian cultural context. The idea and practice of Sufism or Sufi culture has multiple, contesting meanings, forms and interpretations in historical, socio-cultural, political contexts. Its contradictory, dynamic and multiple meanings seem to explain Sufism as a shifting, trans-positioning, ever-hanging cultural construct and practice. In Indian cultural, historical context, the Sufi heritage knowledge production and music practice is recognized to have originated from local, indigenous plural religious traditions and cultures i.e. Bhakti devotional movement, Guru Nanak's Sikh tradition, Buddhism and Hindu Sanatan Dharma. In this context, the cultural transfer, exchange, translation and transposition of ideas and practices seem to underpin the defining feature of Sufi cultural narrative and practice. This also helps to understand the dynamic, collaborating, connecting and trans-cultural conceptualizations of culture.

Both as a transgressive form of mysticism and as a network-oriented organizational phenomenon, Sufism has proven to be intricately trans-cultural also in its recent history. One research was concerned with the transnational and cultural New Religious Movement "Universal Sufism". This movement is characterized by global travel activities and exchange of ideas of the founder Hazrat Inayat Khan as well as of his followers ever since. The research has focused on the centennial celebration of the founder's 'emigration to the West.' The event was celebrated in Delhi's shrine area of Nizamuddin. Furthermore, Islamic sermons were studied as a trans-cultural medium in different contexts. A particular focus has been laid on Egypt and Bangladesh.

The world is witness to a continuous increase in global communications among political and economic philosophies, physical sciences, social sciences and inevitably among religions. This has therefore forced the different religions of the world to come together, which has led to increased communication and understanding, if not unity, of the religions of the world. *"They must develop a spirit of comprehension which will break down prejudice and misunderstanding and bind them together as a varied expression of a single truth"*.

Sufi saints in Maharashtra have historically mediated between Hindu and Muslim believers by performing powerful healing miracles that continue as ritual healing within their shrines and Dargahs today, creating a collective consciousness about the saint among 'patients' and devotees that is benevolent and deeply powerful. Sufi saints and shrines along with their oral tradition and hagiographies form an elaborate layer of regional Islamic history that is associated with trans-cultural genealogies and at the same time came to define regional Islam in Maharashtra as Sufi. Sufi shrines and healing has hitherto been viewed only in a limited manner: as an expression of syncretism and composite culture.

Spiritual health is part of the expression of total human well-being. The sense of being comfortable with oneself and at the same time recognizing that there is an otherness finds an echo in Abraham Maslow's hierarchy of human needs. At each stage of Maslow's triangle, there is a process of change and although the pyramid is often interpreted chronologically, we may operate at different levels at different times. If there are any unresolved tensions remaining in any stage then under stress we 'regress' back to an earlier stage.

This pyramid also illustrates a hierarchy of religious needs and people in spiritual crisis might also be regressing in their religious needs. Addressing the spiritual needs or religious needs of sick people may in the first place be a matter of addressing the most pressing, rather than the most profound. It may be that a person is dying but in the instance of a meeting may most pressingly need to be assured that they are safe, valued or loved. Thus setting out to achieve spiritual health for yourself, or for others must always be needs driven.

Fig 1. *Maslow's hierarchy of needs*

We operate from different levels at different times but many of us have a level where we are 'living' much of the time. If the requirements of the level are met, there is the possibility of progress to the level above. To be sustained, the lower level(s) needs to be met otherwise we regress to it under stress. Spiritual health is, like physical health, relative and never perfect. Indications of perceived spiritual wellbeing are to be found in perhaps surprising places.

True religion is part of being spiritually healthy and individuals may express their spirituality in overly religious terms. True religion, as Peter Speck reminds us, is made up of three parts, theology, religious observance and spirituality. Those who are neurotic are at least still in touch with reality. Religious delusion on the other hand is a false belief, which is not open to logical correction. Even however in the most grandiose of religious delusions, even when someone tells you that they are Jesus Christ, or Muhammad the Prophet (Blessed be they), we may still see flashes of the 'real' person beyond the delusion. It has to be said, however, that ample evidence exists in the behaviours of 'religious' sects, and especially their leaders, to warn us that true spiritual health is achieved, sometimes without formal religion and always without religiosity.

The last decades have been an era of increase in research on Sufism and dervish culture. However, most studies deal with aspects of Sufism within its 'classical', historical context (Buckley 1992, Hammarlund/Olsson/Özdalga 2000). Some of these, nevertheless, consider the outreach of historical Sufism into modern times, such as some contributions in Lifchez 1992 and Silverstein 2010. Others deal with the re-establishment of more or less 'traditional' or 'classical' Dervish order (*tarikat*) structures and rituals, mainly in terms of religious politics *vis-à-vis* movements of political Islam

(Geaves 2006, Toprakyaran 2005). The new role of such forms of Sufism is analysed either in the country of origin, for example in Turkey (Atacan 1990, Neubauer 2008, on female Sufis esp. Raudvere 2002 and Neubauer 2009), or in 'the West' (Westerlund 2004, Malik / Hinnells 2006). Few researchers have explicitly focussed on hybrid (Hermansen 2000), transnational (Werbner 2003, Spellman 2004) transcultural/globalised (Raudvere / Stenberg 2009), or postmodern forms of Sufism and their connections to Western esoteric trends (Taji-Farouki 2009). A major historical watershed is obviously the invention of modern forms of transportation and communication, which has increased the possible degrees of 'transculturation'.

### Oruç Güvenç:

Eminent musician with an interest in historical healing practices at Anatolian*türbe*s (saintly tombs), especially in the different 'sanctuaries' (*makam*) of Karacaahmet Sultan in Western Anatolia, an Anatolian saint from the Middle Ages, also revered much by modern Alevis living in Istanbul. The significant aspect here is the interaction of the use of cultural resources such as material or intangible heritage and traditions and collective practices in processes of identity and group reproduction and formation.

Recently, he organised a conference on "Regenerative Medicine and Spirituality: From Heart to Medicine, From Medicine to Heart". This conference involved a wide spectrum of politicians, Sufis, Turkish as well as European, medical doctors and academics, therapists, health activists, and even Muslim theologians.

Besides 'Sufi Journeys' organised by TÜMATA, Oruç Güvenç and his wife organise smaller tours with Turkish followers. If there is an opportunity, they stage TÜMATA for a concert in local contexts such as town halls or recreation centres. At religiously significant places, such as *türbes*, Oruç Güvenç not only holds concerts together with his followers but also alternatively sometimes switches into the role of an ethnographic researcher, collecting interviews with local people in order to research historic 'healing practices' at the locations.

"Wirbeltanz-Nacht" ('whirling dance night'). The event took place in a middle-sized university lecture hall after an evening concert of TÜMATA from around 11 p.m. until around 6.30 in the morning. The hall was emptied of chairs between the concert and the nightly ritual. The low stage used already for the public concert was also the place for the musicians, which played during the ritual night, around twelve persons from the TÜMATA group plus some other pupils of Güvenç, mostly from Germany, Austria, possibly also from other European countries. Later in the night, also one of the local Sufi musicians from the Sufi Centre "Gayanshala" (Mannheim, Germany) joined in. Most of the active musical participants were dressed more or less 'oriental', or 'dervish-like' or 'shamanic', from complete dress like Oruç Güvenç (wearing for example a Kirgiz hat and an embroidered dress from Central Asia) to only a cap or the like. The guest participants—around forty people—were sitting in a wide circle around the *meydan* ('square'), the middle space left free and later used for the *sema* dance ritual. Only some of the women were covering their hair with a shawl or scarf. As the organiser told me, most of them are one way or the other attached to the healing and therapy business.

Oruç Güvenç gave a short introduction and a kind of 'crash course' in *sema*, translated from the French by his wife Azize. This was illustrated by one of his 'disciples', who showed the basic moves and postures, from 'prostration' (*niyaz*) and kissing the *meydan* up to how to start the whirling, with closed arms first and then unfolding, one palm up the other down, until ending the ritual dance by 'greeting' the ritual leader and again doing *niyaz*. He also advised all the participants to take part in the *zikir* by singing along the songs when they are not dancing. It was interesting that Azize usually translated "Allah" as 'die Göttlichkeit', 'the divinity', which is a gender-neutral expression in German. Altogether, this introductory part took around twenty minutes.

Güvenç started the ritual proper by pronouncing the *fatiha*, the first *surah* of the *Qur'an*. He advised the participants to pronounce the prayer, verse by verse, by repeating his words, which most of them did. Following the *fatiha*, he initiated a first kind of *zikir* with the repeated expression "estaðfirullah", which he calls "a *mantra*". It is the common Islamic formula for repentance, pronounced rhythmically on two pitches by moving the head from right to left for several minutes. In an effective way, this *zikir* brought the group in a common mood of bodily and audio-visual perception. Güvenç ended this rite by pronouncing "estaðfirullah" in a higher pitch.

*Tevhid* is the confession of the oneness of God, such as in the general Islamic confession 'There is (...)

35He took the dervish flute (*ney*) and initiated a second *zikir* hymn which repeats the words "hu, hu, huva'llah" ('he, he, he is God'). Almost immediately one woman from the circle of disciples entered the *meydan* and started to 'whirl'. Other musicians accompanied Oruç Güvenç with frame drums and later by *oud*; then he switched to a kind of *rebab* (oriental 'spike fiddle'). In addition, his wife Azize stepped on the *meydan* and started to whirl. The next tune was a kind of *tevhid* hymn with the refrain "la ilahe illa'llah" in a faster mood. Now, several people stepped on the *meydan* to whirl, including a boy approximately ten years of age. He seemed to be well acquainted with the procedure, as he did *niyaz* while entering and while leaving the *meydan* without hesitation. Several other attendants practiced a sitting *zikir*, moving their bodies in a circling move back and forth. The hymn had Turkish verses, which were sung mainly by TÜMATA members or otherwise well-rehearsed disciples. Some participants—already at this early stage of the ritual—practiced a kind of breathing technique releasing rhythmically their breath pronouncing markedly the "i" of "illa'llah" or uttering "hü" (or 'hu', the Arabic pronunciation *versus* 'hü' in Turkish). The *oud* player had switched to a *kanun* (trapeze zither), and other *oud* players had stepped in. During the course of the night, the different instrumentalists, who also took a break from time to time, changed instruments many times.

The hymns are by no means all classical *zikir* hymns or *ilahi*s (hymns in the praise of god), let alone typical *Mevleviye* pieces for the *sema*. To the contrary, the repertoire, like in his concerts, is composed of songs in the style of classical Turkish music as well as folk songs, which are in key, mode and melody more adjustable to Western culturally modelled audio perception. However, the texts in the majority show God related, 'religious' topics and verses and usually are in Turkish, with occasional exceptions in German. It is noteworthy that songs with texts dominate the repertoire of Oruç Güvenç for accompanying *sema* dance. Actually, almost the complete TUMATA repertoire consists of songs with vocal singing whereas more contemplative solely instrumental parts, as in other Sufi contexts (including Mevlevi), are missing. In this context, we can observe transference from other Sufi and Islamic contexts (sung *zikir* hymns, *ilahi*s) into the *Mevlevi sema*, which then mainly is realised by the whirling, but not in other 'traditional' forms such as classical Mevlevi music, singing, specific instruments of the Mevlevi orchestra, or dress.

However, even more obvious transfer processes take place when one Austrian disciple introduces German Language *ilahi*s. Some are obviously translated from Turkish, when the style of the music remains 'oriental'. Some are in German with a consciously pronounced Austrian accent in the style of Austrian folk songs, but having Islamic texts (with refrains such as "Allah hu" or "la ilahe illa'llah"), especially one praising the prophet Muhammad and another one for "Mevlana" (i. e. the patron of the Mevlevi order, Celaluddin Rumi). Some of these songs are completely "Western" except for the Islamic texts and the fact that they are played on an *oud*; however, even the *oud* then is played like a Western folk guitar. Despite this fact, startling to the observer, the participants continued their whirling or *zikir* moves without much irritation (although there is some laugh towards the unconsciously comical appearance of an Islamic Austrian folk song; mainly the organiser seems to be a little bit annoyed). To the contrary, the fact of 'Austrian *ilahi*s' seems to contribute to the adaptability of the 'strange', 'alien' ritual. Generally, even 'oriental' songs are realised in many cases in a more 'Westernised' style concerning melody, intervals, and harmony, especially when 'polyphony' (or rather homophony, in the sense of chordal singing, versus monophony)—normally unknown to classical oriental music—is introduced, mainly by the realisation of the same melody in different pitches by different singers. In the concrete case observed, it was usually a major third interval, which is known not from classical European music but from 'old-European' folk music, such as Celtic music. This shows an acquaintance of some of the musicians with other musical forms related to contemporary Western esotericism. This fact enables a strong participation by people socialised into the Western musical system in the ritual by singing along 'familiar' melodies and keys without problems. The kind of *zikir* hymns often used by TÜMATA is possibly influenced by styles established by early introducers of Sufi music and Sufism into the West, mainly from Indian origin, such as Inayat Khan.

Turkish novices might be attracted by the utilisation of standard sing-along Turkish folk songs such as "Üsküdar'a Gider Ýken". Interestingly, during the ritual night a much more 'Sufi-like' atmosphere and 'tuning' is brought in by the German Turkish Sufi musician from the Mannheim Sufi Centre "Gayanshala", when he steps in later at night with his *ney* and later with *oud* and voice. He is *inter alia* singing a *deyiþ* (religious hymn, literally 'saying') with a text from Nesimi, a 15th century poet, whose texts are much esteemed and sung by Anatolian Alevis. An additional transference is the introduction of a round dance style *sema*, which is clearly derived from recently much publicised and mediatised Anatolian Alevi ritual. It is realised with expressive breathing sounds in the rhythm of the dance steps, which is not known from standard Alevi ritual. It has to be noted that Oruç Güvenç has a mainstream Sunni background (albeit with Sufi specification) without any explicitly documented contacts to Alevi circles to my knowledge. (However, he surely is aware of the 'Alevi revival'; there is actually—looking at this material and comparing it to modern Alevi rituals by the Alevi *CEM Vakfý* organisation that include *Mevlevi sema*s and*Mevlevi* dervishes—a competition over Sufi forms, especially over the Mevlevi*sema*. Large public

Alevi *cem* rituals with the participation of Mevlevis dancing*sema* were organised by the *CEM Vakfý* for example in Ýstanbul, Ankara or Malatya during the last years.)

In any case, it is remarkable how the group, led by Oruç Güvenç, keeps up a kind of flow the whole night. This is due to his ability to adapt and realise very different styles and modes on a variety of instruments. Additionally, he has obviously established a kind of standard repertoire and sufficient basic abilities in playing, singing and dancing within the core group of his disciples responsible for the uninterrupted conduction of the ritual event. This helps to get over the inevitable moments of tiredness and boredom during the long hours of the night. Although some participants fall asleep, there are always enough people actively participating so that no real breakup of the ritual occurs. Oruç Güvenç closes the ritual by initiating a joint "hu" and a long prayer of plea and blessing, in French, with some core terms that he leaves in Turkish, translated by his wife into German. Then, he leads the ritual community in praying the *fatiha* together. At the very end, he shakes hands with the musicians sitting next to him and advises them to repeat this handshake of reconciliation with all the members of the ritual community. Lastly, the organiser, who announces the communal breakfast following the ritual, gives a speech of gratitude and announces a following workshop by Oruç Güvenç. Whereas the concert had a (moderate) fee, the whirling night was free; however, donations were expected. The main income for the 'professional' musicians therefore possibly is the fee for workshops, usually held during the days before or after the *sema* rituals or a concert, where paying pupils are educated in oriental instruments and ritual dance techniques.

## Conclusion

The flexibility to react to very different circumstances and audiences in 'Western' as well as 'Oriental' contexts shows Oruç Güvenç's ability as a musical performer, knowing how to design a program for an event, to select appropriate pieces and to improvise; an ability also demonstrated by some of his followers. This is an interactive process, however. There are some standard core practices and canonical musical pieces in his rituals. This fact gives the somewhat individualistic and of course eclectic and syncretistic practice of Oruç Güvenç a certain continuity and establishes a tradition of a fluctuating group, centred on him and his German wife Andrea Azize.

For the discussion in the academic field of 'musical therapy', see Oberegelsbacher; Timmermann 199 (...)

The ritual forms are the result of different transfer processes of ritual elements from different traditions: Central Asian, classical Sufi music and dance, Western folk music, to name some of them. Thus, the Sufi ritual of Oruç Güvenç is a system of practices constructed via many processes of reception and accommodation. It can be described as an eclectic system of practice, thought and discourse. However, it forms a system 'in its own right', as every ritual performative practice linked to a committed "community of practice" does. It is a master example of extreme ritual dynamics, which enables its adaptability from rural Anatolian up to urban Turkish or Western contexts. In light of recent research in the Research Centre "Ritual Dynamics" (University of Heidelberg, Germany) on 'ritual design' (see Karolewski et al. 2012), it could also be stated that Oruç Güvenç can be called an unconscious ritual designer. Unconscious, because he is determined to uncover age-old systems of effective practice, while at the same time creating very new forms of fluctuating "communities of practice" (Stausberg 2001). He is, however, conscious of the need to adapt to different audiences. His large repertoire of different musical styles, instrumentations and personnel allows him to do that without having to feel opportunistic. Rather, he sees himself as integrating different, but related cultural resources that are connected to his general aim: to provide a framework for therapeutic healing. This is the perspective of an ethnographer and historian of religion. As aspects of healing efficacy lie out of the scope of my research and outside my expertise, I cannot evaluate the possible effectiveness of the practices involved. Nevertheless, in terms of ritual as a mode of human expression and identity building, they seem to be highly effective in several ways.

**From Self to Self:**

Many Sufi poets compare consciousness to a cup and unconsciousness to the ocean, individually we are like the cup but all of us together with nature are the ocean, unconscious reality, or God. If we have the ability to lose the limitation of the cup by freeing the self we can be reunited with the ocean of being, which would enable us to lose the anxieties of separation, loneliness and isolation and gain the permanency of the everlasting ocean.

In the path of Sufism a Salik (traveler) must go through seven stages of nafs (self) in order to reach the essential self, the self that is merged with the divine. According to Fadiman & Frager the lowest level of self is the commanding self, which is the selfish and evil self. The regretful self is able to at times discriminate between right and wrong and resist temptations. These first two are more or less under control of the false self. The inspired self is interested in spiritual knowledge and is compassionate. This is the highest stage that conventional religion can attain. The contented self is the beginning of the loss of ego and attachments, which is followed by the pleased self that has accepted good and bad as things from God and submits to reality. The sixth stage is the self pleasing to God, which is in total submission to God; they have reached the 'inner marriage of self and soul'. The final stage is the pure self, the soul of perfection where there is no self left, it is the complete human being, it is the divine.

"The self is not bad in itself. Never blame your self. Part of the work of Sufism is to change the state of your self. The lowest state is that of being completely dominated by your wants and desires. The next state is to struggle with yourself, to seek to act according to reason and higher ideals and to criticize yourself when you fail. A much higher state is to be satisfied with whatever God provides for you, whether it means comfort or discomfort, fulfillment of physical needs or not."Sheikh Muzaffar

Rumi illuminates this state for us:

If you could get rid
Of yourself just once,
The secret of secrets
Would open to you.
The face of the unknown,
Hidden beyond the universe
Would appear on the
Mirror of your perception

**References:**

Louis, K., 1990. Empathy, anxiety and transcultural nursing. Nursing Standard, Nursing Standard 5, S.

Maslow, A.H., 1970. Motivation and Personality. Harper Row, New York.

Speck, P., 1988. Being There.. SPCK, London.

# TOURISM MARKETING : GLOBAL TRENDS

**Overview**

There have been significant realignments in tourism decision patterns and roles within the industry, as a result of global economic, political, and social changes and the impact of new communications technologies. As in some other sectors of society, these technologies appear to be encourage a greater decentralization of distribution, greater individual access to choice and information, and a realignment of roles for tourism intermediaries. An easily recognizable trend is major opportunities for tourism industry participants who provide value as "experts", respond to demand for individualized service, fulfill higher level needs and aspirations of tourists ("fulfillment", "self-actualization", "individuality"), and remain flexible and responsive to change. Sustainable tourism projects and products are especially well poised to take advantage of these changes, to provide unique value to tourists, and to spread the benefits of responsible tourism to new areas and a wider segment of the host population.

### Tourism, global security and the economic picture

Security and economic concerns are still significant factors affecting travel decisions, globally and across demographic sectors. Continued currency value realignment (particularly the reduced value of the US dollar against the Euro) will continue to shape consumer and industry spending decisions. Tourists, overall, are not curtailing their travel, so much as spending less (tourism receipts have decreased more than have the number of international arrivals), and staying closer to home. This has led to an increase in regional and local tourism. Regional budget airline growth is also fueling this trend (The continued viability of their business models remains to be seen, however).

Major new outbound markets are developing in China, India, Russia and other ex-Soviet countries, and to a lesser extent, the Middle East, as a result of economic and social changes in these countries. The Asian markets among these are tending to produce mostly regional travel demand, which should help Asian tourism rebound from losses in previous years.

### New pressures and new roles

The global security and economic situation remains volatile, and rapid technological innovation looks to remain the norm. Wider availability of new communications technologies will change tourism markets in ways not yet imagined. Flexibility, diversification, and decentralization seem certain to become more important for the survival and success of tourism organizations and tourism-based economies.

Internet travel purchases (now the largest amount of all online purchases) and airline competition have led to a downward pressure on prices and slimmer profit margins for tour operators, travel agents, and throughout much of the industry; in general, leading to necessary realignments within the industry.

More competing tourism products, decreased customer loyalty, and increases in last-minute booking present challenges to tourism organizations. They will need to work harder to differentiate their products and services, help tourists sort through the "information clutter", engender trust and loyalty, and maintain stable revenue flows.

Smart marketers appear capable of countering the above trends and displacing price's centrality in purchase decisions for some types of travel products. More sophisticated uses of these new communication technologies, such as Internet-enabled customer relationship management tools and email marketing campaigns, would allow for more selective marketing and distribution strategies to attract highly desirable tourists.

Internet and other new communications tools are displacing some tourism intermediaries and redefining the roles of others. Tourism product suppliers are less reliant on traditional distribution intermediaries, and consumers are more willing to make their own travel arrangements. The WTO notes that the current emphasis on regional travel is also producing less group travel and more individual travel (people feel more confident to make their own arrangements, when the destinations are more familiar).

Trust is more than ever a central concern for travel purchasers. By nature, the product cannot be tried before purchase, and businesses on the Web must still overcome a healthy skepticism about the trustworthiness of the companies and offers they discover online. Speedy decision-making is also important, as the most frequent travelers are often also the most pressed for time; particularly as the number of competing tourism choices threatens to overwhelm their ability to choose.

There is an important opportunity for "experts" to support decision-making about tourism purchases. Agents and intermediaries which add real value with their specialist expertise and personal service will remain relevant and successfully navigate the shifting roles in travel distribution.

### New demand and opportunities for sustainable tourism

Even the smallest operators, like community-based tourism groups, can generate their own demand. Where distributors remain necessary, they can negotiate distribution from a position of greater strength, and reduce price pressure on their tourism products.

While price pressures and competition have characterized most parts of the industry, there has been sustained or increased demand for luxury accommodations, tours, and other travel packages. The trends are not mutually exclusive within one set of purchase decisions: "Luxury travelers" may choose budget transportation, expensive accommodations, and adventure tours (which might previously have been seen as incongruous choices). More consumer access to information, better product customization, and more attention to demand-led marketing are both revealing and producing more complex travel purchase habits. The "package holiday" approach to tourism products may be on its way out. An increase (2-3% from 1993-2003) in tour customizations may be related to this trend toward individualization.

Active travelers have not been deterred by security concerns, but have also traveled more regionally. Self-identified "active travelers" intend to increase travel expenditures over the next few years. According to the World Tourism Organization, "active travelers" rate available activities higher than destination in terms of importance to their purchase decisions. ecotourism, nature tourism, hard adventure, soft adventure, sports tourism, and health tourism count among the top growth sectors. For example, the World Tourism Organization estimates that the market for nature tourism is increasing at 6 times the rate of tourism overall.

There appears to be evidence for a "self-actualization" dividend (if not a "green dividend") for tourism sales. There are signs of increasing interest in travel for reasons of personal growth, assertion of individuality, human connection, and "authentic experience", among segments of major outbound markets. These segments overlap markets for "luxury experience" and new, "exotic", "individual" consumer goods. These travelers appear more flexible about price ("price elastic"), when they can be convinced that an experience offers significant additional value (in terms of the interests listed above).

These consumer and lifestyle groups have been called "Cultural Creatives" in the USA; "New Authentics", "Style-Lifers" and "Neo-consumers" in Europe (the groups and findings represented by these terms are not totally interchangeable, but appear to overlap more than not on characteristics important to tourism decisions). As an example of these groups' significance: the original research done about "Cultural Creatives" showed they represent 25% of the adult U.S. population at the time of the study—the polling group American Lives estimates that they amount to 50 million people including both the U.S.A. and Europe.

The desirability of market segments which use travel consciously as a means of personal growth and a defining "lifestyle accessory" will lead to increased use of "lifestyle marketing" through partnerships with producers of psychologically-associated products and related organizations. These tourists require different marketing approaches; they appear not to respond well to direct marketing, for example; are avid media consumers; and tend to require corroboration of information from a trusted authority or personal acquaintance.

Sustainable tourism products are poised to take advantage of the preceding trends, as lifestyle products in line with the demand for organic foods, Fair Trade products, and "natural health-care", all "luxury," "individual", and "authentic" products, of demonstrated appeal to people in these "new lifestyle" groups.

Sustainability is of increasing concern to tourism organizations of all sectors. The effort at "greening" tourism is now the focus of hundreds of initiatives and conferences, as well as certification efforts, worldwide. Many of the largest institutional donors have recognized its validity and value as an approach and a goal, and include sustainability as a central criterion in their development packages—and major donors are increasingly turning to tourism development to achieve overall development goals.

Sustainability will increase in importance as a central part of donor organizations' project goals, project recommendations, and donation criteria. Economic viability, as a component of sustainability and project value, will be of increasing concern to the donors.

# IMPACTS OF TOURISM DEVELOPMENT

Tourism is one of the world's largest and fastest growing industries. It is also one of the important sectors of the Indian economy, with great potential for income generation and employment. India has been ranked as one of the fastest growing travel and tourism economies in the world. This industry is the fastest growing foreign exchange earner in India and stands high in terms of income generation. As per World Travel and Tourism Council (WTTC) statistics, tourism in India is poised to grow at a rate of 8% per annum till 2016. Poon (1993) noted: "The tourism industry is in a crisis – a crisis of change and uncertainty; a crisis brought on by the rapidly changing nature of the tourism industry itself." The industry is in metamorphosis – it is undergoing rapid and radical change. New technology, more experienced consumers, global economic restructuring and environmental limits to growth are only some of the challenges facing industry.

Infrastructure is an important determinant of productivity, development, and poverty reduction both within borders and across them. Increases in income and overall national growth create new, greater demands for better infrastructure-based services, such as transport, telecommunications, energy, water supply and sanitation. These services are important for both fueling and sustaining growth of a destination, which is vital to tourism development. In turn, national growth can contribute to regional security and economic development - so long as the cross-border infrastructure is in place to support integration, such as airports, ports, tunnels and roads. For Asia and the Pacific to experience this kind of growth, it needs to gain ground on two fronts: institutional coordination and physical investments. Infrastructure investment is entering a new stage, marked by new operators and sources of capital, a redefining of the public sector's role, and new instruments for regulating and overseeing public services. The role of the private sector, whether through public-private partnerships (PPP), private sector participation, is becoming increasingly important.

Along with tourism infrastructure development and an increase in the number of travelers, there is a simultaneous increase in the potential for both positive and negative impacts. Technological advancement, innovations and a changing travel market have affected all segments of the economy and simultaneously provoked new concerns in terms of social and environmental issues. There is a need to analyse the various impacts of tourism development.

**Economic Impact:**

The purchases of travellers coming from outside the host community brings in new revenues from external sources. The expenditures of travellers also increase the general level of economic activity in the host community in various ways. Visitor expenditures in a community are considered exports as the products and services are sold to people from outside the host community. Imports are regarded as leakages as money leaves an area to purchase outside resources.

· *Faculty Member, Indian Institute of Tourism Travel Management, An organization of Ministry of Tourism, Govt. of India, Bhubaneswar, Odisha, India*

**Direct and Secondary Effects:**

In order to measure the actual economic impact of tourism on a community, it should be emphasized that a host community may not actually receive all travel expenditures. For example, payment for air transportation is usually made at the traveller's point of origin and does not accrue to the destination. Other examples include payments for imported food, beverages, and retail products. While travellers may consume or purchase these products during their stay, these payments leave the host community and represent a debit to the community's trade account

The amount of visitor expenditures that remains in a community provides a source of income for residents and businesses. Visitor expenditures received as income by businesses such as hotels, restaurants, car rentals, tour operators, and retail shops serving tourists have a direct effect on the economy of the host community. Indirect or secondary effects come about as the money received by support services and other local businesses are used in turn to pay for supplies, wages of workers, and other items used in producing the products or direct services purchased by the visitors. A visitor creates additional income for many sectors of the economy. By generating new jobs and, in many cases, new businesses, tourism can affect the distribution of income in a community. The redistribution of income may have both economic and social impacts, depending upon the pattern of ownership and availability of local resources.

### Tourism Multiplier:

The term multiplier is used to describe the total effect, that is, both direct and secondary, of an external source of income introduced into an economy. The concept of the multiplier typically is used in the travel industry to encompass the direct and secondary effects of visitor expenditures on an economy.

Multipliers can be estimated for sales or output produced by businesses, employment, payroll, or other variables. The value of multipliers will not be the same for all countries or communities depending on the availability of local resources in the respective areas. Island communities with limited resources, for instance, may lose 50% or more of their visitor expenditures as direct payments for imports of all kinds-construction materials, textiles, food, etc.-and therefore have lower multipliers as exemplified in the low multipliers for Dominica, Antigua, and especially the Cayman Islands.

### Price Changes:

The prices of products and services can change in response to changes in demand and/or supply conditions. Lower production costs can result in lower prices for the respective products and services. Higher prices can result from an increase in demand or increases in production costs. Visitor spending in a host community may result in higher prices because their purchases would increase the demand for goods and services. This leads to an inflationary situation, whereby residents would also have to pay more for goods and services which are in demand by both visitors and residents. Through the multiplier, prices of other goods and services may also increase as income in the community increases and people want more goods and services. Rising land values caused by tourism development is also a major contributor to inflation. As prime land in scenic locations is acquired for resort, recreation, or attraction development, land prices are bid up in surrounding areas for commercial or residential purposes. Improvements – infrastructural and building enhancements – increase property value and tax bases, which are ultimately reflected in prices passed on to consumers.

**Economic Instability:**

Pleasure travel, as a discretionary item, is subject to fluctuations in travel prices and income of travelers. Because of these fluctuations, a host community's growth may be unstable. Periods of rapid growth, static growth, and declines put an economy that is heavily dependent on tourism on shaky ground. Natural disasters such as volcanic eruption, hurricanes and floods are unpredictable. These disasters have destroyed communities and discouraged travel to affected areas. Tourism is also sensitive to acts of terrorism, outbreaks of disease, and other unfavorable conditions which put the economy of a host community at risk.

**Social Impact:**

The social implications of tourism development are complex .The most obvious social impacts are also economic ones. These relate to the creation of new jobs and the influx of new income to the area. Although such jobs are usually analyzed in terms of economic benefits, their social implications cannot be overlooked. Although economic impacts can be quantified, many of the studies on social impacts measure perceived impacts. This is also true for studies on cultural and environmental impacts, since it is difficult and in some cases impossible to measure actual social, cultural, or environmental impacts.

**Employment and Migration:**

New opportunities for employment created by tourism are not only visible to residents; they also can attract new migrants to the host community. As a result, the question arises as to whether or not these newcomers actually fit into the community. An example is provided by the People's Republic of China, where thousands of migrant workers were drawn from the rural areas to such already overcrowded cities as Shanghai, Beijing, Xian, and other places where new hotels and resorts were being built to meet visitor needs during the booming decade of the '80s.

To understand the social impacts of a growing population, it is necessary to examine such factors as the arrival of new migrants. The faster a community is required to assimilate new residents, the greater the stress on the present structure of the community. Another aspect to consider is the fact that tourism may create job dislocations in other sectors. This may prove to be detrimental to established industries, such as agriculture or fisheries in the area, when workers choose to work in tourism and abandon jobs in agriculture or other industries which are perceived as being less rewarding. These dislocations may disrupt a community's economy built on agriculture or other traditional industries.

Many of the jobs created by the travel industry do not require high-level skills. However, as the travel industry matures in specific destinations, the number of skilled and professional jobs generally increases. While lower-level positions may be easy to fill, positions that require specialized managerial and technical skills are often difficult to fill in communities with technical or professional skills shortages. As a result, the better-paid and higher-status jobs tend to be held by outsiders. In order for a community to fully benefit from tourism, decision makers must include measures to educate and train local residents for higher positions; to ignore this problem is to invite inevitable community resentment and subsequent government intervention.

**Traditional Role of Women:**
Women in the workforce are today a common phenomena of modem industrialized countries; but there are still many countries and communities in the world where women occupy traditional homemaking roles. As travellers seek new or less frequented destinations, tourism is being developed in some of the places where conventional family structures and social values remain unchanged. The conservative social structure of these communities which have opened to tourism may be disrupted when women enter the work force for the first time. The case of the Mauna Kea Beach Resort on the island of Hawaii illustrates what can happen when tourism is introduced into a traditional community. Frances Cottington, psychiatrist, and Mary H. Smith, sociologist, in separate studies examined the first-time employment of large numbers of women when the luxury-class Mauna Kea Beach Resort opened on the rural North Kohala coast of the Island of Hawaii in the late 1960s. At that time, the island's economy centered around rural plantations, mainly sugar and pineapple. Men were the sole

breadwinners in these agricultural communities. The Mauna Kea Beach Resort was the North Kohala area's first entry into the tourist industry. The opening of tourism employment opportunities to plantation women, however, stirred unexpected conflicts and tensions in the rural lifestyle and family social order.

Cottington's conclusions were essentially negative, citing the following:
- loss of self-respect among husbands of working women who, in some cases, began to earn more than their husbands or who became the sole family support as men were laid off by local sugar plantation closings;
- jealousy of some husbands whose wives had to dress up "glamorously" to serve hotel guests;
- increased divorce rates, crime, and juvenile delinquency;
- frustration and financial insolvency *from* rising expectations and subsequent over-spending by workers exposed to high consumption patterns of hotel guests;
- increased anxiety and illness among females who were unaccustomed to and unprepared for the increased pressures and responsibilities of working for the first time.

Smith, in a paper written three years later, acknowledging the validity of Cottington's observations, tentatively concluded that the hotel's "culture shock" on the community was subsiding somewhat and that the benefits were beginning to outweigh the negative effects. She cited these examples:
- increased family income visibly raised the standard of living in the community;
- new skills and salaries gave women workers a sense of increased self-worth and accomplishment;
- expanded social contacts with fellow employees and

tourists produced an expanded awareness of the outside world among the women workers;
- family roles were changing for the better as husbands assumed more of the household and child-rearing chores;
- husbands were beginning to develop more respect for their wives as competent individuals able to hold good jobs;
- increased income and an expanded world view could result in more opportunity for higher education for the workers' children.

Consequently, although initial effects of tourism appeared to be negative, the long term effects seem to be beneficial for the women and their families.

### Consumption Behaviour:

From a sociological perspective, tourist expenditures can have both a positive and negative effect on a community. When business is good, the additional revenues generated by visitors raise the general level of income in the community, which in turn raises the standard of living for residents. On the obverse side, when residents begin to emulate the lifestyles of outsiders, their own values and consumption behaviour may change, shifting from conservative consumption patterns towards the instant gratification of wants and desires. Residents of rural communities quickly observe that their own locally produced consumer goods are often inferior to imported goods. As a result, residents begin to save less and borrow more in order to support altered consumption habits.

### Sociological Cycle:

Analogous to the life cycle theory of a destination, tourist destination development from a sociological perspective follows five basic phases: (1) discovery stage, (2) developmental stage, (3) conflict stage, (4) confrontation stage, and (5) decline stage.

The discovery stage is noted for its low volume of visitors, and hence, residents are not exposed to any of the effects of development. Residents welcome tourism development enthusiastically in the development stage, because of its visible contribution to the local economy. Benefits are perceived in terms of improved infrastructure and higher income levels generated directly by tourism or tourist-related jobs. However, development also encourages crime as visitors become visible prey for perpetrators and juvenile mischief makers.

Local resentment first appears in the conflict stage, which is reflected in hostile attitudes toward visitors. This hostility usually results from competition over resources- water, energy, land usage, recreational facilities, beach front property, and so on. This can be perceived positively when acknowledged as a means of preserving open space and reducing overall development densities. However, problems arise when residents are excluded from such facilities or when a resort developed primarily for visitors cramps the traditional leisure activities of residents.

Problems are further accentuated in the confrontation stage, which results in organized opposition to new developments, land use rights, and fights over the use of scarce resources. The decline stage is usually signalled by hostile activities, such as forms of sabotage, rampant crime, lack of safety, and outflow of capital. The last three stages are attended by a progressive erosion of community goodwill; once goodwill and community support are gone, the consequences are difficult, if not impossible, to reverse.

It is essential that these social phases be understood in

order to prevent, or at least deter the erosion; social planning is one of the viable means to do so effectively. Research on the social consequences of tourism on the community is the first step. The information generated by research should lead to an action plan to circumvent possible unfavourable social impacts and to reinforce tourism's positive contributions. Second, it is mandatory that the community be involved in the actual planning and development process. Residents should be made to feel that they have a stake in the success of the destination.

Social planning is necessary at all levels of development- for mature as well as new tourism destinations. Mature destinations are more susceptible to social deterioration when destinations become saturated, markets dissipate, and new investments are not forthcoming. Planning efforts at this point must be focused on halting the erosion process, although the measures taken may not always be successful.

## CULTURAL IMPACT

The impact of tourism development on culture is difficult to assess. Tourism development creates an economic demand for the trappings of local culture. The demand cultivated by tourism provides opportunities, good and bad, to preserve or exploit local art forms and customs. On the positive side, local artists, musicians, craftsmen, and individuals engaged in the performing arts are able to make a living in their crafts and vocations, thus helping to keep the arts alive and well in the community. This core *of* employed artists can spark a general renewal *of* interest by residents in their own cultural heritage.

On the negative side, selling or performing for pay on a regular basis *of* what was once done ceremonially or to perpetuate a tradition, can break down the cultural value and respect *of* local residents for their own art forms, religion, and traditions. These cultural displays, which once were ends in themselves, now become just a means *of* achieving a different end-earned cash income.

Some sociologists believe that tourism in its less benign form is nothing short *of* an invitation to a collision *of* cultures and values - an opening for a direct confrontation between people with vastly differing values and social patterns.

## Cultural Collision:

When cultural collision occurs, several results are possible:

1. *Accommodation*, or more accurately "toleration," in which both the visitor and the visited coexist in a live and let live fashion;

2. *Segregation* in which the tourists and host population maintain a social distance or separation by means *of* either avoidance or containment *of* visitors within luxury hotels, golf courses, shops and other amenities designed for tourists;

3. *Opposition* in which the tourists are rejected by members *of* the host community or, the host community is rejected by tourists who behave in a condescending manner toward residents or ridicule local customs, lifestyles, vocabulary, or speech;

4. *Diffusion* in which either or both groups, the tourists and the host population, borrow or adapt cultural traits or elements of the other.

In earlier times, these processes were activated only through migration, colonization, religious proselytization, political occupation, or inter-regional trading. Today, with increasingly efficient modes of transportation and numerous package tours, tourism has stimulated contact between people of varying cultures as never before. Thus, tourism has become an agent of, as well as an impediment to, cultural change.

In the United States, the invasion of Lancaster County, Pennsylvania by tourists has all but extinguished the unique and fragile way of life of the Amish and plastered the once-tranquil countryside with motels, gas stations, golf courses, drive-ins, frozen custard stands, souvenir shops, and an amusement park. An Amish farm bakery, once noted for its shoo-fly pie, is now selling canned, homemade pizza sauce. Tour bus visitors, all with the determination of amateur lens enthusiasts on a photo safari, subject horrified Amish children to "forced photography." The children have been raised to believe that a photograph is a graven image and equate being photographed with breaking the second of the Ten Commandments.

**Cultural Interpretation:**

Cultural or **community interpretation** is one means of mitigating the negative impacts of tourism upon a host region's culture. One of the main objectives of cultural interpretation is to assist visitors in developing a keener awareness, appreciation, and understanding of the area and culture of the people they are visiting. Before this can be achieved, it often is necessary to first educate residents about the area within which they live.

The general goal of community interpretation is to link people with sites, stories, and information about an area, as well as to link people with other people in a community and residents with visitors. Effective interpretation relates a site or subject matter to everyday life and presents information from unique viewpoints to stimulate thinking. The environment can be used in terms of sound, smell, taste, and touch to arouse visitors' curiosity and interest in learning.

The better informed visitors are about a place and its people, the more respect and sensitivity they will have toward them. Community interpretation also provides a more enriching experience for" visitors and helps them to differentiate one destination from another. For residents, community interpretation enriches their understanding and also provides a means for preserving the cultural integrity of an area.

## ENVIRONMENTAL IMPACT

The environmental impact of tourism development is a basic issue that must be considered whether in a developed or a developing country or community. In a developing community, tourism can be an answer to some of the prevalent life-threatening environmental problems, such as poor water supplies, inadequate sanitation and sewage facilities, deficient nutrition, bad housing conditions, sickness and disease, and vulnerability to natural disasters. In a developed community, on the other hand, these fundamental environmental problems for the most part already have been solved, but secondary environmental problems, such as congestion, waste disposal, pollution and other side effects of growth become mounting issues.

In addition to the natural environment, the human environment as it relates to people must also be considered. The objectives of sustainable tourism recognizes the importance of balancing economic goals within the constraints of both the natural and human environments.

### Natural Environment:

In a developed community the problems of urbanization- human and vehicular traffic, congestion, noise, exhaust fumes, air pollution, sewage, loss of green belts, and other detriments can destroy the pleasant ambiance of the community for visitors and residents alike. One means of combatting environmental pollution is to control a community's rate of development.

Even as the impact of tourism is undergoing closer scrutiny, there is also growing awareness of the importance of the environment to tourism. In far too many communities, unfortunately, the awareness has come at the eleventh hour, when damage has already been done to both the environment and the tourism industry. In many coastal and lakeside areas around the world, pollution from resort communities, along with industrial waste of nearby factories and plants, have rendered waters so polluted and toxic that warning signs must be posted to alert tourists not to swim or fish from these waters.

The Galapagos Islands is an example of a destination that is essential to science and to the tourist economy of Ecuador. These islands are an isolated archipelago 600 miles west of Ecuador in the Pacific with unique species of wildlife, both flora and fauna. Because of the importance of these islands for natural science study and the need to guard against the adverse effects of unrestrained human intrusion on wildlife, the Ecuador government devised a way to use controlled tourism as a means of raising funds to save the environment and to establish protected areas. Controlled tourism in this instance required a working definition of the carrying capacity of the Galapagos and limiting the number of visitors to a safe level in order to protect the wildlife and ecology of the islands.

**Human Environment:**

Human environment is the environment as it relates to people. It embraces factors that are physical, psychological, and ecological. Beauty, harmonic proportion, and naturalness are qualitative elements of these factors. Changes in the physical environment should be made with the objective of creating a destination that is pleasing to visitors, yet that blends into, or further enhances, the natural landscape. Developers attempt to accomplish this objective by promoting the use of organic materials, low-rise architecture, and landscaping design that complements the natural advantages of scenic sites. Another means of enhancing or preserving the human environment is to maintain the historical and/or cultural integrity of an area. Tourism offers many opportunities for bringing people and their heritage together, thus building a bridge between past and present.

At present, the long-range environmental effects of tourism development vary greatly from one location to another, depending on a host of variables, including physical characteristics of the site, historical land use patterns, and the type of visitor facilities proposed. What is known, however, is that environmental effects must be considered in the planning process, since tourism development (as does any kind of land or industrial development) alters the landscape and the ecological balance of living things. The environment, which is such an important part of an area's attraction, is fragile and too easily destroyed if responsible planning is neglected.

**Tourism Development in Odisha:**

The infrastructure for tourism development exists in two categories, i.e. Basic and Touristic. Road, electricity, water, external and internal transport, postal and telecommunication, medical care, etc. constitute basic facilities; accommodation, restaurant, public convenience, organised tours, recreation and guide service, etc. constitute touristic facilities. Availability of basic facilities is a prerequisite for creation of touristic facilities.

Ever since its creation, OTDC has been managing the tourist facilities pertaining to accommodation and transport The Department of Tourism has continued its efforts to create and operate new tourist facilities to attract budget tourists. The involvement of private entrepreneurs to maintain and manage tourism units on lease is noteworthy.

A number of tourism projects have been taken up as a part of infrastructure development:

- Special Tourism Area
  Land acquisition for development of Special Tourism Area between Puri and Chilika was expedited.
- Peace Park at Dhauli
  Foundation stone was laid for establishment of an international standard Peace Park at Dhauli as part of the development of the Buddhist Circuit in Odisha.
- Guide Training Programme
  Tourist Guides have been trained under the CBSP programme conducted by the joint collaboration of Indian Institute of Tourism and Travel Management and Odisha Tourism.
- Safety & Security of Tourists
  Home Guards have been deployed on the Puri Beach for ensuring safety and security of tourists. Likewise, several aggressive strategies have been formulated for enhancing promotion and publicity:
- Promotion Campaign
  Odisha Tourism organizes Publicity campaigns and Road Shows at different places within and outside the country for generating awareness.
- Publications

Tourism Publications like well-designed and informative brochures on Chandaka, Eco-Tourism Guideline, Chilika Boat race, Kalinga Mahotsav, Raja Festival, Konark and many other publications on different districts have been brought out.
- Advertisements
  Attractive and innovative advertisements. were released in several periodicals & dailies for promoting Odisha as a Tourist Destination.
- Website
  The Odisha Tourism Website is constantly updated and refurbished to focus on the tourism products of the State.
- Fairs & festivals
  Odisha Tourism has regularly participated in Tourism Festivals for promoting and giving a face-lift to Odisha as a preferred tourist destination.

While Konark Festival is organized by Department of Tourism, the Chilika Boat Race is organized by CDA, Naval Training Centre, Balugaon and Odisha Tourism; festivals like Folk Festival at Sambalpur, Parab ( Tribal Festival) at Koraput, Chhau Festival at Baripada, Beach Festival at Chandipur, Kalinga Mahotsav at Dhauli, Kharvela Mahotsav at Khandagiri, Srikshetra Mahostav at Puri, etc. are financially supported and promoted at national and international level.

**COSTS AND BENEFITS OF TOURISM DEVELOPMENT**

All actions that accompany or result from the decision-making process of tourism development have various alternative impacts on costs and benefits from economic, social, and environmental standpoints. It is important to keep in mind that tourism development is, above all other considerations, an economic process. Social and environmental issues become irrelevant if tourism does not prove to be economically viable.

To measure the economic and other impacts of tourism, a cost-benefit analysis may be undertaken to weigh the benefits from tourism. Factors taken into account for this analysis include revenue, foreign exchange, employment, household income, taxes, and other benefits against the costs. of investments. Also considered are the use of various resources, including land, water, displaced labor, infrastructural support, social services, etc., needed for tourism development. For maturing destinations with saturated markets, depreciating assets and high marketing expenses, the costs may begin to equal or exceed benefits. In the case of newer destinations with growing market demand and modest investment requirements, there will be an opposite 'experience of greater benefits than costs, The cost-benefit concept is important for policy-makers and investors who consider making trade-off decisions when weighing the consequences of development alternatives.

### Capital Investment Costs

When considering the cost of tourism development, one must recognize the extensive investments required of both government and private capital to finance the preliminary planning and development stages. Further, it requires extensive capital investments in fixed assets and tends to offer a low rate of return on investment during the early years of operations.

Examples of capital investments for tourism structures include:
- infrastructure-airports and other types of transportation terminals, roads, and land improvements;
- transportation systems and equipment;
- accommodations-luxury, medium-quality, and budget;

- food and beverage establishments;
- cultural institutions-museums, theaters, and galleries;
- exhibition and convention centers;
- recreation and sporting facilities;
- retail shopping facilities;
- theme parks, amusement centres and other attractions;
- historic preservations and restorations.

## Social and Cultural Costs

Other aspects of the cost of tourism development are the social and cultural costs. The list is long and includes the following:

- additional demands on social services and supporting infrastructure;
- costs of creating new jobs;
- costs of creating and maintaining positive community relationships;
- psychological costs to the employees related to the disparity between their own lifestyle and that enjoyed by visitors;
- costs of possible friction between visitors and local residents over shared usage of valued local recreational facilities;
- opportunity costs to the community of spending limited public capital for support of infrastructure, rather than for other projects of potentially greater direct benefit;
- quality of life costs of increased stresses on employees' home lives and unanticipated lifestyle changes;
- cultural costs of alterations in locally espoused ceremonial or traditional values;
- loss of privacy in rural communities where tourism development occurs.

**Environmental Costs**

Another aspect of costs is environmental costs:
- increased levels of generalized congestion and pollution;
- alterations to the natural landscape and changes in the ecological balance of living things;
- costs of preventing localized congestion or pollution;
- costs of the loss of wilderness areas or inevitable degree of lessening the natural attraction;
- costs of creating conservation areas on resort lands;
- costs of undertaking enhancement projects, including unforeseen or undesirable side effects;
- costs of undertaking historical or cultural preservation.

**Benefits**

On the benefit side, tourism development provides employment and revenue to support local business in the community. Sophisticated infrastructure systems required by tourism development often benefit the community by encouraging and serving economic development in other industrial sectors. The daily contact of residents with visitors may broaden educational and cultural horizons, improve feelings of self-worth, and promote upward mobility and acquisition of material advantages. New revenue generated by tourism also has a social benefit for the community in terms of improvements in the quality of life related to a higher level of income and improved standards of living.

The interest of visitors in local culture provides employment for artists, musicians, and other performing artists and often tends to revive the community's interest in its own cultural heritage. Philanthropic programs and educational and cultural interchanges sponsored by travel businesses also have a social benefit.

Environmentally, tourism development in under developed regions with scarce raw material resources generally solves or ameliorates prevalent life-threatening environmental problems. In developed regions, recreational land set-asides preserve open space and reduce overall development densities. Because the natural attraction is so important to the long-term economic viability of a destination, tourism development often includes conservation of endangered species of flora and fauna, enhancement of the natural and human environments, and historical and cultural preservation projects- all of which have direct or indirect benefits to the surrounding community.

**References:**
- Turner, L. "Tourism – The Most Subversive Industry". New York : Hill and Wang, 1973.
- Gee, C. Y. "Sustainable Tourism Development : A Strategic Issue for the Asia-Pacific Region".Kuala Lumpur, 1994.
- "Trends in Travel and Tourism Expenditures in U.S. Measured Media – 1989-1991, Ogilvy and Mather, 1994
- Jones, Evan. "Asia Travel Trade", September, 1994
- Nolan, Jr., S.D. " Variations in Travel Behaviour and Cultural Impact".San Francisco, 1975

# FESTIVAL TOURISM AND CULTURE

## Introduction

Festivals have been defined as cultural forms of and about 'culture' (Bauman 1986); cultural performances allowing to enact and celebrate the multiple symbolic elements which add sense and meaning to the various oppositions and discontinuities of everyday life (Singer 1959).Festivals have long been considered the traditional cultural activity of any region. Festivals are the crystallization of culture, spiritual and physical activities which have been chosen, maintained and improved over many generations. Festivals are the living cultural museums of the ways people live their lives.

Festivals and special events are one of the fastest growing types of tourism attractions. Even in small towns of less then one thousand people, it is not uncommon to see two or three major festivals held per year (England, 1994).Because of their proliferation and the magnitude of some of these events ,it has been suggested that festivals and special events are one of the three major categories of tourism attractions(Getz,1991).As such festivals and special events can compete the other types of ambient attractions

,such as climate, scenery, wild life, permanent attractions,etc.

Odisha's intriguing festivals and events speak of the state's cultural affluence. Marked by colour and gaiety, these festivals and events are often associated with legends, myths, and even day to day rituals. Every region has its own set of distinctive celebrations that pepper almost all months of the year. In addition to the regional and religious festivals the Odisha tourism departments endeavor to showcase the fascinating traditions of art and culture of the state by organizing several special events is praiseworthy. Characterised by joyful celebrations, each of these festivals accompanies Odisha's unique ways of life, culture, and creative accomplishments. The objective is to keep alive the ancient Odishan culture, as well as to create an awareness and appreciation for it amongst the masses. The organizers want the society to realize how traditional heritage can be developed and beautifully presented, without disturbing the glorious historical base and spiritual remifications.Also, the endeavor is to promote and popularize Orassan art and culture in various forays, at national and international level.

**Culture**

Culture is an important but can be a slippery, even a chaotic, concept. It can mean a great deal when its scope and relevance are clearly defined and yet also very little, especially when it is used as synonymous for 'the social'. To assert that culture is central does not mean that everything else is secondary. When we consider the possible meanings, connotations and uses of the word 'culture', we face a mass of interpretations and symbolic associations. How are we to make sense of this concept? It is at one and the same time a mark of distinction and of assumptions upon which such distinctions are forged. To study cultural things is an activity which often refers to the exploration of the practices and lifestyles of the elite in a particular society, of high culture ,yet it can also involve the investigation of the live experiences and representation of everyday life as in 'class cultures','ethinic cultures' ,'street cultures' ,even 'subcultures' and 'club cultures'(Thornton 1995) Culture has been called "the way of life for an entire society." As such, it includes codes of manners, dress, language, religion, rituals, norms of behaviour and systems of belief. Various definitions of culture reflect differing theories for understanding — or criteria for evaluating — human activity.

Sir Edward B. Tylor writing from the perspective of social anthropology in the U.K. in the late nineteenth century described culture in the following way:

"Culture or civilization, taken in its wide ethnographic sense, is that complex whole which includes knowledge, belief, art, morals, law, custom, and any other capabilities and habits acquired by man as a member of society." More recently, the United Nations Economic, Social and Cultural Organization UNESCO (2002) described culture as follows:

"... culture should be regarded as the set of distinctive spiritual, material, intellectual and emotional features of society or a social group, and that it encompasses, in addition to art and literature, lifestyles, ways of living together, value systems, traditions and beliefs".

While these two definitions cover a range of meaning, they do not exhaust the many uses of the term "culture." In 1952 Alfred Kroeber and Clyde Kluckhohn compiled a list of more than 200 definitions of "culture" in Culture: A Critical Review of Concepts and Definitions

These definitions, and many others, provide a catalog of the elements of culture. The items catalogued (e.g., a law, a stone tool, a marriage) each have an existence and life-line of their own. They come into space-time at one set of coordinates and go out of it another. While here, they change, so that one may speak of the evolution of the law or the tool. A culture, then, is by definition at least, a set of cultural objects. Anthropologist Leslie White asked: What sort of objects are they? Are they physical objects? Mental objects? Both? Metaphors? Symbols? Reifications? In Science of Culture, (1949), he concluded that they are objects "sui generis," i.e., of their own kind. In trying to define that kind, he hit upon a previously unrealized aspect of symbolization, which he called "the symbolate," i.e., an object created by the act of symbolization. He thus defined culture as: "symbolates understood in an extra-somatic context." The key to this definition is the discovery of the symbolate.

In this globalised world of us every region, more or less, looks feels and behaves the same. This threat of loss is making us reconsider how significant is our cultural heritage as an express ion of what we are. Cultural activities create meanings and thus are concerned with and embody the identity and values of a place. Culture matters not only because it represents the anthropological image of the material, spiritual and social life of people, but also because it is basic resource for sustainable economic growth. Defined in its broadest sense, the notion of culture encompasses a wide range of idiosyntric meanings:historic, political, legal, technicological and artistic. Culture is a critical aspect of mediating and articulating community need, as development is planned and take shape through cultures potential to empower and animate.

Increasing competition between regions, cities and places for resources to support development is placing increasing emphasis on culture as a source of differentition,inspiration and narrative. "Tourists who take in cultural activities while traveling outside their home communities are considered cultural tourists. These people do not necessarily define cultural activity as their primary motivation for travel. For instance, a business traveler who catches a play is considered a cultural tourist. The umbrella term cultural tourism includes performing arts, visual arts, heritage, **multicultural/ethnic events**, and some attractions, but is not limited to these areas."

### Culture, festivals and special events

Festivals have been defined as cultural forms of and about 'culture' (Bauman 1986); cultural performances allowing to enact and celebrate the multiple symbolic elements which add sense and meaning to the various oppositions and discontinuities of everyday life (Singer 1959).Festivals have long been considered the traditional cultural activity of any region. Festivals are the crystallization of culture, spiritual and physical activities which have been chosen, maintained and improved over many generations. Festivals are the living cultural museums of the ways people live their lives.

Indian festivals and celebrations are an integral part of the Indian culture with special social and religious significances and are major unifying elements in the country of many differences.

The word fest derives from the Middle English, from Middle French word festivus, from the Latin word festivus. Festival was first recorded as a noun in 1589. Before it had been used as an adjective from the fourteenth century, meaning to celebrate a church holiday. The etymology of feast is very similar to that of festival. The word "feste" (one letter different from "fest") comes from Middle English, from Middle French, from the Latin word festa. Feast first came into usage as a noun circa 1200, and feast was used as a verb circa 1300.

Festivals and special events are characterized by a **specific theme** designed to **attract spectators** or visitors to a **specific location** where they are invited to **participate, learn, watch, and enjoy** a temporally limited and spatially confined occurrence.

A festival or fest is an event, usually staged by a local community, which centers on some theme, sometimes on some unique aspect of the community. Among many religions, a feast or festival is a set of celebrations in honour of God or gods. A feast and a festival are historically interchangeable. However, the term "feast" has also entered common secular parlance as a slang term for any large or elaborate meal. When used as in the meaning of a festival, most often refers to a religious festival rather than a film or art festival.

### Types of festivals

Seasonal festivals- Seasonal festivals are determined by the solar and the lunar calendars and by the cycle of the seasons. The changing of the season was celebrated because of its effect on food supply.

**Arts festival-** An arts festival, also art festival, is a festival that focuses on the visual arts. Notable festivals include the Adelaide Festival of Arts in Adelaide, South Australia and the Singapore Arts Festival.

**Film festival-** A film festival is a festival in one or more movie theaters with a special program showcasing many films. The films are usually of a recent date; sometimes there is a focus on a specific genre or subject . These are typically annual events.

**Food festival-** A food festival is a festival, usually held annually, that uses food, often produce, as its central theme. The largest one in the United States is the Taste of Chicago in Chicago, Illinois.

**Literary festival-** A literary festival, also known as a book festival or writers' festival, is a regular gathering of writers and readers, typically on an annual basis in a particular city. A literary festival usually features a variety of presentations and readings by authors, as well as other events, delivered over a period of several days, with the primary objectives of promoting the authors' books and fostering a love of literature and writing.Writers' conferences, although similar to literary festivals, are sometimes designed to provide an intellectual and academic focus for groups of writers without the involvement of the general public.

**Mela Festival-** Mela Festival are the multicultural events which have their roots in the traditional Asian Mela. Mela can mean Market or Event or Religious Gathering etc: its origin is in the moment where crowds gather. They are distinguished by their bringing together of Asian and Native cultures, to produce a multicultural event from the perspective of the Asian communities. Mela Festivals are celebrated with music, dance, theatre, fashion, food and stalls

Music festival- A music festival is a festival that presents a number of musical performances usually tied together through a theme or genre.

New Age Festival – Festivals relating to the New Age have been popular through-out North America since the late 1980s, promoting alternative spiritual lifestyles. They cater mostly to those interested in subjects such as channelling, meditation, reincarnation, crystals, psychics, holistic health, environmentalism, and New Thought. Typically these events offer an environment wherein the public can explore many and varied subjects, experience various alternative therapies, consult with psychics and attend lectures, workshops and seminars

Religious festival – A religious festival is a time of special importance marked by adherents to that religion. Religious festivals are commonly celebrated on reoccurring cycles in a calendar year or lunar calendar. This means that, because ancient calendars were not hugely accurate, the exact date of the festival changes each year.

Theatre festival- Theatre festivals are amongst the earliest types of festival. Classical Greek theatre was associated with religious festivals dedicated to Dionysus. The medieval mystery plays were presented at the major Christian feasts. The Theatre as an everyday part of life is a comparatively recent phenomenon. In recent years theatre festivals have been established to promote various types of theatre, such as the works of William Shakespeare and George Bernard Shaw. Many festivals, such as those in the fringe theatre movement promote the work of beginning playwrights and performers.

## Festival Tourism and its impact

Festival Tourism was termed 'an emerging giant' over 10 years ago (Getz & Frisby, 1988: 22) but even now there appears to be a relatively small and disparate literature on the subject. Most frequently used as a 'catchall 'term to include special event tourism and festivals of any size or organizational persuasion, festival tourism makes a complex topic of study that has been tackled from a variety of perspectives.

Festivals and events are a very crucial part of the tourism industry and can play a tremendous role in the growth and development of a destination. They can attract visitors, and make the streets safer, revitalize the evening economy and create a stylish ambianc Overall it may have the following impacts- -symbolic benefits relating to the image of a destination. -economic benefits -physical and environmental impacts -social benefits -community development -leisure participation -boosting cultural tourism Events can help brand a destination and provide a catalyst to attract visitors who in turn spend money in the region that would not have occurred had it not been for the event. An event can act as a deciding factor by differentiating one destination from another ,even resulting in the time change of visits to coincide with the staging of an event, which can be described as the 'time switching factor'. Festivals and events can encourage tourists to extend their stay in the host destination in order to include it in their itinerary or further their travel after the completion of the event. Festivals and events can act on a long term basis to stimulate repeat visitation because tourist may return to the destination for more extensive travel, once they have had a sample of the environment.

In the long term, festivals and events assist in the development of a destination's image as well as instill a sense of pride amongst the host population.

The timing of an event can also serve as an additional leverage tool. Given the seasonality of the destination, festivals and events can be utilized to boost tourism in peak as well as in lean seasons.

Cultural activities can have a tremendous impact in

the development of a destination. In Europe, Barcelona engineered its revival through an ambitious cultural programme linking urban design, the creation of new cultural flagships and cultural festivals and events.

Glaslow, an old industrial city, reinvented itself as a stylish and glamorous destination through investment in culture—and there by attracted international companies to locate there.

Festivals can extend the tourist season, generate revenue for governments (Ritchie & Beliveau, 1974), and have 'positive economic impacts on the local economy' by generating income, supporting existing businesses and encouraging new start-ups (Mitchell & Wall, 1986: 140). Mitchell and Wall's study found that smaller festivals produced most economic benefit but that as festivals became more established the economic impact became relatively less significant.

Although these authors were researching the economic benefit in a relatively narrow sense, they suggest that a greater balance between economic and community benefit is desirable in countering local resistance to festival growth.

They note '. . . the influx of additional tourists results in a change in community infrastructure to serve the needs of festival visitors'(ibid: 140)so that, as festivals grow and begin to make stronger links outside the locality, local entrepreneurs are likely to become 'resentful' and that consequently the economic benefits of the festival become less significant.

Illustrating this point, research on the economic impact of the internationally famous Brecon Jazz Festival reportedly confirms its income generating properties. However, almost simultaneously, reports of local businesses' growing dissatisfaction with the festival's 'impact on town life' over the festival period began to appear. News items on local businesses closing for the duration of festival and of local retailers' 'growing unhappiness' with its impact on their livelihood were reported in the run-up to the event. Concern over the future of Brecon Jazz culminated in 2001 with the withdrawal of sponsorship by long-standing supporters Hyder Group and British Airways. In a similar vein, the world famous Glastonbury Festival was cancelled in 2001 reportedly due to concerns over exceeding the capacity of the site. The population of the Mendip region doubles during the festival and there were doubts about the ability of essential services (police, fire, hospitals) to cope in an emergency. Residents make regular complaints to Mendip Council regarding the invasion of visitors to the area and concerns over the safety of festival-goers include the potential for mass dehydration and food poisoning . Such reports surrounding apparently 'successful' and 'internationally acclaimed' festivals must be a causefor concern to organisers everywhere.

Though economic impact studies continue to suggest that festival tourism can benefit local tourism-related businesses income generation alone is not enough. If festival tourism is to contribute to sustainable localities it is reasonable to suggest that a spread of benefits for residents and business should be sought. For communities living on marginal incomes, being able to pay for a college education on car parking fees or being able to raise $14,000in 10 days by selling fudge is 'too significant to be ignored' (Janniskee & Drews).

A hypothetical 'social multiplier' has been developed to explain the ways in which festival tourism contributes to increased 'organisational activity' in a locality (Getz, 1984) bringing improved leadership, improved local accountability, better public–private co-operation and the investment of profits back into the community.

Festivals are often intimately related to the maintenance and celebration of community values and ultimately, to their survival. Local festivals are said to be celebrations of community and effectively to serve as a public demonstration of 'what a community is all about' (Falassi, 1987:). It is also argued that although few rural festivals are about 'money-making' many play an important role in generating a visitor industry for their host communities (Janniskee & Drews, 1998:).

Visitors to rural festivals are often from urban centres and bring economic benefits to local shops, restaurants, hoteliers, craft producers, entertainers and all manner of goods and service providers in the festival area. Such festivals are considered a success if they provide 'wholesome fun' and cover expenses, but they are also meant to: raise funds for service organisations, put money in the pockets of local vendors, provide a showcase for local talent, create a positive image of the host community, instil community pride, promote clean-ups and fix-ups and make business sponsors happy. (Mayerfield & Crompton, 1995: 41).

In a similar vein and in the context of the 'blossoming' of festivals in rural America, it is claimed that festivals attract tourists who might otherwise never visit and that: as a delightful bonus, the beneficial side effects of festivals extend well beyond generating tourism dollars and include strengthening rural communities and enriching the quality of small town life. (Janniskee & Drews) In addition to the social positives it is also notable that examples of environmental improvements may be found at festival locations. As festival time approaches, residents will become involved in activities that make the locality more presentable

(Janniskee,). Over time, motivation and money is generated for community improvement projects such as 'redeveloping down- towns, preserving and restoring historic buildings, renovating old theatres, constructing parks and community centres, planting trees, paving streets and installing holiday decorations' (ibid: 395). While environmental negatives may occur from a transport perspective, an advantage of festivals is that they are temporarily-short lived and, with effective planning, are unlikely to pose the problems for the community that 'year round' tourists might. This link between tourism and environmental preservation and conservation has long been recog- nised (Bramwell & Lane; Mathieson & Wall; Stewart,).

There is some evidence to suggest that festival tourism, with its links to community development and concern for local environments, could be said to be one of the most sustainable forms of tourism development, as its very nature demands a balanced approach.

## Local Economic Development and Sustainability

Early attempts to measure development concentrated on economic growth demonstrated as rate of change of GDP per head, but in recent years there has been a trend toward a greater consideration of socio-economic and environ- mental variables. This has often been encapsulated within the elusive term 'quality of life'. While current notions of development usually *incorporate* economic growth they are not necessarily the same thing. Economic growth can occur simultaneously with increases in poverty, unemployment and inequality (Binns, 1995; Warburton, 1998). Therefore it is argued that development is concerned with the human betterment that may be achieved by improvements in lifestyles and opportunities (Binns, 1995:

305–6). Eisenschitz and Gough (1993) have traced the burgeoning of local economic development activities in western economies and note the commonality between them: . . . across this variety there is a widely shared framework: the need for local control of the economy, the use of indigenous resources, the promotion of enterprise and the mobilization of community co-operation. These are seen as key to the health or revival of local economies, and indeed as important means to national economic regeneration. (1994: 3–4) Arguably, despite the variety, three distinct approaches to local economic development can still be identified: 'conventional economic development', 'community economic development', and 'sustainable economic development' (Bingham & Mier, 1993). The conventional approach emphasises policies which operate within the formal economy through such measures as inward investment and promotion, the building and management of industrial workspaces, assisting new sectors of growth and supporting training schemes (see e.g. Blakely, 1989). Community economic development focuses on the interface between the informal and formal economies and promotes the 'well-being' of the community it serves. The latter approach can be either complementary to the conventional approach or an alter- native to it.

'More sustainable' forms of local economic development involve consider- ation of the 'longer term' and 'inter-generational equity'. Notions of 'carrying capacity' and 'balance' (social, economic and environmental) are common, fostering participation and community ownership of initiatives (Richards & Hall, 2000; Warburton, 1998). These acknowledge the need for a shift in the way localities operate and imply a need for changes in lifestyles. Sustainable local economic development is not, as yet, a checklist of activities or policies to be 'ticked off' when achieved, but the work is ongoing. An example would be the attempts being made to develop frameworks which allow local authorities or other responsible bodies to audit and review their progress towards the implementation of sustainable tourism.new ways of thinking about the sustainability continuum are developing and there is some evidence of a convergence of ideas around sustainable approaches to local economic development that makes links to all aspects of a locality. As awareness of the concept of sustainable local economic development has increased, there is a recognition that economic growth alone is 'not enough' (see Tony Blair PM's foreword to the DETR Sustainable Development Strategy for the UK, 1999). Despite such high level support for the concept there remains less agreement on how it might be achieved.

Many organisations(public, private, voluntary and cross-sector partnerships) are actively seeking ways to implement sustainable forms of development at the local level. One such is the charity Forum for the Future which seeks to find ways to 'improve the lot' of local economies. This organization works to push forward the boundaries of understanding by taking a 'positive, solutions oriented approach' to sustainable development (Forum for the Future).

The event organisers do not take into account the social and environmental impact in to consideration. It is argued that there is a clear need to adopt a holistic approach:

In any location, harmony must be sought between the needs of the visitor, the place and the host community (English Heritage,). Host communities play a major role when running a major sporting event or any other large scale events. Also, major sporting events play a major role in host communities.

The work of Getz (1997) was concerned with the event manager gaining support and resources from the host community, while also looking at the local benefits and costs, cultural meanings of their event and also the political factors. If all this is taken into consideration then it can lead to a good event and even a good relationship between event and local community. A problem a host community may have with the event is the influx of people and it being unable to cope. This may have a knock on effect in terms of traffic congestion, crime and vandalism. Also Smith (1989) tells of how the socio-cultural impacts result from the interaction between 'hosts' and 'guests'. A number of factors may contribute to difficulties in this relationship. The transitory nature of a visit to a historic centre may be too short to allow any understanding to be established. Repeat visits may be more positive in this context. Visitors, especially those on day visits, have temporal constraints and become more intolerant of 'wasting time', for example in finding somewhere to park. Spontaneity may break down as 'hospitality' becomes a repetitive transaction for the host (Glasson et al 1995, pp.34-5). However they can intern have increased tourism over the time of the event, then due to the exposure, have short-term or long-term tourism due to the attention the event has been given.

The impacts of events can greatly affect the quality of life of the local residents. Therefore, it is been argued to adopt strategies to take into control the social and environmental impacts of festivals into analysis when carrying out economic impact of the each individual event. The event organisers only take into consideration the economic implications and ignore the resident perceptions, which provide important non-economic dimension for gauging how events benefit or impinge on the host community

(Jeong and Faulkner, 1996; Hall, 1992). The festivals have a number of impacts arose on the host city, ranging from cultural, economic, social and environmental. Festivals have both positive and negative impacts on their host cities, but emphasis is often focused on the economic analysis. Hall (1992) suggests that the ability of major events perceived to attract economic benefits of events often provide the official justification for the hosting events. Economic analysis of events provides one aspect of why events are held and the effects that they have on a region. However, while many of the economics impacts of events are quite tangible many of the social are not. (Hall, 1992 p.10)

The full assessment of economic impact must also take into account other aspects. The benefits sought by the development of the cultural tourism through festivals are similar to the economic roles of events defined by Getz (1997). Getz believes that: The full assessment of economic impact must also take into account other aspects. The benefits sought by the development of the cultural tourism through festivals are similar to the economic roles of events defined by Getz (1997). Getz believes that:

"The economic role of events is to act as catalysts for attracting visitors and increasing their average spend and length of stay. They are also seen as image-makers for the destination, creating a profile for destinations, positioning them in the market and providing a competitive marketing advantage." "The economic role of events is to act as catalysts for attracting visitors and increasing their average spend and length of stay. They are also seen as image-makers for the destination, creating a profile for destinations, positioning them in the market and providing a competitive marketing advantage."

According to Getz (1997) economic impact assessments often include a multiplier calculation to demonstrate that incremental tourist expenditure has direct, indirect and induced benefits for the local economy. At the most basic level, economic impact analysis techniques estimate average per-person spending, multiplied by the total number of visitors/users to determine the direct spending associated and then apply multipliers to estimate secondary or indirect economic effects. The multiplier usually used in tourism impact studies is the "income multiplier" which is basically a coefficient which expresses the amount of income generated in an area by an additional unit of tourist spending.

Tourism is considered of value in economic development for its considerable income generating properties and its ability to provide jobs (Williams & Shaw, 1998: 6). Despite this the benefits of tourism have been challenged as concern over tourism's wider negative tourism and the implications of these for sustainability have become more clearly .

Moreover, sustainable **tourism** itself remains a contested concept. The tensions around sustainable **tourism** remain despite its promotion at the highest level, and what has been described as a 'rigid acceptance that the principles and objectives of sustainable development can easily be transposed onto most **tourism** develop- ment contexts' (Inskeep, 1991: xviii). In spite of the continuing vigorous debate it seems reasonable to suggest that a favourable symbiosis between certain types of **tourism**, such as **festival tourism**, and sustainable development may exist.

**Festivals and culture tourism**
**The Impact of Festivals on Cultural Tourism**
Today festivals are considered to contribute

significantly to the cultural and economic development wealth of the host destination. The festivals have major impact on the development of cultural tourism to the host communities. The festival organisers are now using the historical and cultural themes to develop the annual events to attract visitors and creating cultural image in the host cities by holding festivals in the community settings. The desire for festivals and events is not specifically designed to address the needs for any one particular group. The hosting of events are often developed because of the tourism and economic opportunities addition to social and cultural benefits. Many researchers have contested that local communities plays vital role in development of tourism through festivals. Events have the potential to generate a vast amount of tourism when they cater to out- of-region visitors, grants, or sponsorships, (Getz, 1997) of direct or indirect intent.

The government now support and promote events as part of their strategies for economic development, nation building and cultural tourism. The events in turn are seen as important tool for attracting visitors and building image within different communities. According to Stiernstrand (1996), the economic impact of tourism arises principally from the consumption of tourism products in a geographical area. According to McDonnell, Allen and O' Toole (1999), tourism related services, which include travel, accommodation, restaurants, shopping are the major beneficiaries of the event. As far as events and tourism is concerned, the roles and responsibilities of governments as well private sector and society in general have significantly changed over the last decade. The situation have been changed where the state had the key responsibility for tourism development and promotion to a world where the public sector is obliged to reinvent itself by relinquishing of its traditional responsibilities and activities in favour of both provincial/ state and local authorities. This indicates the growing influence on the behaviour of governments and business in general of development of event and tourism industries. This suggests that festivals impact on the host population and stakeholders in a number of ways. These factors are primarily concerned with social and cultural, physical and environmental, political and economic impacts, and can be both positive and negative. Community based events and festivals provide an opportunity for the celebration of local identity and community empowerment and create tourism for the local area.

**Cultural Tourism**

Cultural tourism is defined by Tourism industry professionals as "Travel directed toward experiencing the arts, heritage and **special** character of a place." The culture is an identity and the importance that individual people place on local and national social organisations, such as local governments, education institutions, religious communities, work and leisure. Cultural tourism describes tourist the once who take part in the cultural activities while away from their home cities. Cultural tourism is that form of tourism whose purpose is to discover heritage sites and cultural monuments on their travels. Garrison Keillor (1995) in an address to the White House Conference on Travel & Tourism, best described cultural tourism by saying,

**"We need to think about cultural tourism because really there is no other kind of tourism. It's what tourism is...People don't come to America for our airports, people**

don't come to America for our hotels, or the recreation facilities....They come for our culture: high culture, low culture, middle culture, right, left, real or imagined — they come here to see America."

The theme of culture has grown over the last two decades but not clear definition of culture has accepted by the community has whole. The culture in modern day is seen as a product by the governments, large organisations and individual people to develop their own standings in the given market. *Wyman states that culture plays important part in the society:*

"...In an economic climate where we hear so much about crisis in health and education, it is important to remember that culture, too, is an essential element of a healthy society. It's not an either-or situation. Health is necessary for life; culture makes life worth living...."

Moreover, cultural tourism relates to those individual groups of people who travel around the world, individual country, local community and individual events that seeks to experience a heritage, religious and art sites to develop knowledge of different communities, way of life. This can include a very wide range of cultural tourist experience. It can include, for example, performing arts, festivals visits to historic sites and monument, education tours, museums, natural heritage sites and religious festivals.

## Development of Cultural Tourism through Festivals

The festivals have changed over the years, before festivals were associated with key calendar moments, linked specifically to particular seasons and heritage sites. Over the last decade these have been changed and developed upon, there is now a broad and diverse range of festivals events taking place all over the world.

Getz (1997) introduces festivals & events as -:

"Events constitute one of the most exciting and fastest growing forms of leisure, business, and tourism-related phenomena."

Goldblatt (2002, p.1) introduces festivals events as a: "Kaleidoscope of planned culture, sport, political, and business occasions: from mega-events like Olympics and World fairs to community festivals; from programs of events at parks and attractions to visits by dignitaries and intergovernmental assembles; from small meetings and parties to huge conventions and competitions."

The revolution in festivals has been stimulated through commercial aspect to meet the changing demand of the local community groups and increasing business opportunities for the events organisations and local businesses. Festivals play a major part in a city and local community. Festivals are attractive to host communities, because it helps to develop local pride and identity for the local people. In addition, festivals have an important role in the national and host community in context of destination planning, enhancing and linking tourism and commerce. Some aspects of this role include: events as image makers, economic impact generators, tourist attractions, overcoming seasonality, contributing to the development of local communities and businesses, and supporting key industrial sectors.

The festival organisers are now using the historical and cultural themes to develop the annual events to attract visitors and creating cultural image in the host cities by holding festivals in the community settings. Festivals provide an opportunity for the local communities to develop and share their culture, which create a sense of values and beliefs held by the individuals in a local community and provide opportunity for members of the local community to exchanges experiences and information. Festivals provide the tourist the opportunity to see how the local communities celebrate their culture and how this effects the community development, it also helps the visitors to interact with the host community and help people to enjoy and meet their leisure needs.

The peoples and communities that host the festival provide the visitors with a vibrant and valuable culture. In addition, culture is the personal expression of community heritage, community perspective, it provides cultural opportunities for the visitors to enjoy and experience local illumination and culture. The festivals also provide support to those who pursue economic opportunity related to sharing community culture with the broader world. UNEP (2002) suggest that the culture tourism is boosted through the development of festivals and events. Tourism can add to the vitality of communities in many ways. One example is that events and festivals of which local residents have been the primary participants and spectators are often rejuvenated and developed in response to tourist interest.

### Cultural events and festivals of Odisha

Akshyaya Trutiya: This is exclusively an agricultural festival held on the third day of the Hindu year. On this day the farmer ceremonially starts sowing seeds in the field, especially paddy. Early in the morning, farmers in their respective homes arrange the materials for the ritual. After taking ablution in a river or tank they wear new clothes and carry the seeds in new baskets, In the field offerings are made to Lakshmi, the Goddess of wealth which the farmers do it themselves. Then they sow seeds ceremonially praying the Goddess for a rich bumper crop. In the evening feasts (strictly vegetarian) are arranged in respective homes. In western Odisha this festival is called 'Muthi Chhuan'. Eating of green-leaves (Shag) is forbidden for the day. It is observed by all farmers irrespective of caste and creed.

The famous Chandan Yatra of Lord Jagannath which is observed in various other shrines of Odisha starts from this day. Moreover, from this auspicious day the carpenters start building the cars (Ratha) of Lord Jagannath, Balabadra and Subhadra.

On this day women also worship 'Sasthi Debi' popularly called 'Sathi Duchhei'. The Goddess is said to be the guardian of children. She has also the power to bestow the women with children. Therefore, she is propitiated with great devotion.

Religious scriptures testify that Ganga, the sacred river of India landed on the Earth on this day from Heaven. She is the perennial source of water which is the need for agriculture. Therefore, this auspicious day was chosen to start sowing seeds.

**Gahma Purnima:** The full-moon day in the month of Shravana (August) is known as Gahma Purnima or Go Purnima. In the Hindu tradition even the animals and plants, who are benificial to the human beings are propitiated. The cow is regarded as mother. So, Gahma Purnima is a festival of the agriculturists to worship the cattle. Bullocks are the most important animals for an agriculturist in India. When ploughing the field with bullocks is over the farmers venerate them for the service they have rendered. Along with the cattle the God of agriculture Baladeva is also worshipped. The religious scriptures testify that Balarama invented the plough and showed the people all methods of agriculture. Therefore, bullock is His vehicle and the plough, His weapon. He has been also taken in as an incarnation of Vishnu in holy scriptures. It is for this reason this festival is also known as Baladeva Puja or Baladeva Jayanti in some areas.

On this day the cattle shed is cleaned and neatly plastered and sketches of bullocks, bullock carts, ploughs and other agricultural implements are drawn on the walls. Bullocks are bathed and decorated with flowers and sandle-paste. Their horns are oiled. The rituals of worship takes place in the cattle-shed itself for which Brahmins are not needed. A piece of new cloth is placed on the back of the bullocks and they are fed with rice-cakes and pulses.

In the afternoon the bullocks are taken to a field where all the agriculturists gather. Each bullock is made to jump over an altar known as Gahma bedi and this portion of the festival is called Gahma dian. It is said that this is reminiscent of similar festival first arranged by Baladeva Himself when He first took the bullocks to plough the land for agriculture.

Though essentially a festival of agriculturists, this festival has other religious and social ceremonies too. The other name of the festival is Rakhi Purnima or Rakshya Purnima. The religious scriptures testify that on this day Kunti, the mother of the Pandavas vested the responsibilites of safety of her sons to Lord Krishna as the Kauravas wanted to kill them. So, the festival goes on from that date and is known as Rakshya Purnima or full-moon day of protection. On this occasion the Brahmins of Odisha go from house to house and bind sacred threads on the wrist of the people invoking Gods to protect their lives. In northern India it is mostly a social festival in which sisters bind sacred threads on the wrists of their brothers to protect them from dishonour. This tradition though new to Odisha is slowly gaining ground.

Though Vaishnavism prevailed in Odisha much earlier,

the cult of Krishna worship was made popular during the 15th century by Sri Chaitanya and his followers. Though temples exclusively dedicated to Krishna are few in Odisha, the representative deity of Lord Jagannath is no other than Krishna known as Madan Mohana, Ramakrishna, Gopala, Gopinatha etc.

To the Vaishnavas the festival is known as Jhulan Purnima or the Swing festival which is observed in most of the Vishnu temples and monasteries following the cult. Beginning from the Tenth day of the bright fort-night, it culminates on the Purnima day. The metal images of Radha and Krishna are placed on beautifully decorated swings and nights are spent with singing and dancing in front of the deities. As an important festival of Lord Jagannath, the celebration of the festival in the shrine and monasteries at Puri attracts visitors from far and near. The festival in the temple was first initiated by the Gajapati king Dibyasingha Dev-II (1793-1798).

**Makara Sankranti:**

The orbit of the Earth round the Sun is known as Kranti Brutta (Circle of Movement). It takes full one year for the Earth to take the orbital move. The orbit is divided into-twelve parts known as 'Rashi' and accordingly the year has twelve months. The day the Earth starts moving from one 'Rashi' to another is called Sankranti and is counted as the first day of the month. Makara Sankranti is the first day of the month of Magha. According to the Christian calendar it generally falls on 13th or 14th of January. It is the day on which the Sun enters the sign of Makara Capricorn) which is the beginning of Uttaravana or the Sun's northern course.

Makara Sankranti as a festival is modestly celebrated other parts of Odisha excepting the districts of Mayurbhanj, Keonjhar and Sundargarh, where it is observed as the most important festival of the year. Almost in every Hindu household 'Makara Chaula', a special variety of dish prepared with raw-rice, molasses, coconut, chhena (cheese), honey and milk etc. is offered to the Sun-God and then taken by all. People in general have early purificatory bath and visit temples. According to the Sun's movement, the days from this day onwards become lengthy and warmer and so the Sun-God is worshipped as a great benefactor.

In the districts of Mayurbhanj, Keonjhar and Sundargarh where the tribal population is more than forty per cent, the festival is celebrated with great joy and merriment. Though this is not a festival of the tribal people, but because of their acculturisation with the Hindus for centuries they have been celebrating this festival with great enthusiasm. Moreover, the time of the festival is best suited for them as all agricultural operations are over by that time and each family possess something after the harvest.

Preparation for the festival starts much earlier. All the houses are cleaned and neatly plastered. They are painted with three colours viz. White, red and black. New clothes are worn by young and the old alike. Sweet cakes and a meal with meat-curry is a must in every household. Liquor is freely consumed by men and women They sing and dance and enjoy life for about a week. Before the day dawns all the, people take their purificatory bath in the river or tank and wear new garments. The day is spent with feasting and merry-making. In some places village-style sports are also organised and there are ram-fighting, cock-fighting and archery competitions. Young girls of certain communities mostly Kudumi, Bastiti, Rajual etc. worship 'Tushu', a female deity and immerse it in the river or tank singing songs of a special variety. In the temple of Lord Jagannath this festival is observed as 'Uttarayana Yatra'. In some places big fairs are also held on this occasion and the biggest of its kind is held at Jagatsinghpur of the Cuttack district.

**Ashokashtami:** This is the car-festival of Lord Shiva celebrated with great enthusiasm at Bhubaneswar and is considered to be the most important festival of Lord Lingaraj. On the eighth day of the month of Chaitra the representative deity of Lingaraj Sri Chandrasekhara is drawn on a car from near the temple to the temple of Rameswara. Thousands of people congregate on this occasion to watch the festival. There is a puranical account about the origin of the festival. It is said that Lord Ramachandra, inspite of all efforts couldn't kill Ravana as Goddess Kali was protecting him. Then he was advised by Bibhisana, the younger brother of Ravana to propitiate the Mother Goddess and win Her support. Then Ramachandra prayed the Goddess for seven long days with elaborate rituals and could please Her to withdraw support from Ravana. When Her favour was withdrawn it became easy for Ramachandra to kill Ravana through 'Brahmastra', the unfailing weapon. To celebrate this victory he took out Shiva and Durga, in a chariot, out of pleasure and satisfaction. From that day the festival is being observed. As the 'shoka' or sorrow of Ramachandra was removed by the death of Ravana, this day is called Ashoka (devoid of shoka) Astami or Ashokastami. Some religious texts are of the opinion that Parvati could get Shiva as Her husband on this day and she became 'Ashoka' (removed off sorrowfulness) and therefore, the festival has been named as Ashokastami.

**Ganesh Chaturthi:** The day dedicated to the worship of Ganesha, the elephant-headed son of Shiva is known as Ganesha Chaturthi which is the fourth day in the light half of the month of Bhadrab. Ganesha, the God of the masses is one among the most important deity in the Hindu pantheon. He is the remover of all obstacles and bestower of success. His elephant head suggests cool-brain and the steed, rat suggests perseverance; the two qualities that are important to achieve success. In the worship of all other Gods, even of His father Shiva, Ganesha is invoked in the beginning. There is no ritual without a prayer to Him. Almost in every important shrine of Odisha Ganesha appears as a Parswa Devata or the guardian deity.

The festival is celebrated with great enthusiasm in all the educational institutions and also in public places. Highly gilded images of the deity are worshipped with great devotion. The business community, especially the shopkeepers preserve an image of Ganesha. They pray to Him daily for their success. On this day they change the image with a new one and immerse the old in a river or tank.

**Nuakhai:** The most important festival of western Odisha comprising the districts of Sambalpur, Bolangir, Sundargarh, Kalahandi and some areas of Phulbani, is Nuakhia. Generally it takes place in the bright half of the month of Bhadrab on an auspicious day fixed by the astrologers. In the ex-State areas the date is fixed according to the instructions of the ruling Chiefs.

The people in general eagerly look forward for the festival and preparation starts before a fortnight. Most of the houses are cleaned, neatly plastered and decorated by the house wives. On this occasion old and young, all wear new clothes. Though the festival is intended for eating new rice of the year, it is observed as a general festival. Meeting of friends and relatives, singing, dancing and merry-making are parts of the festival. On this occasion the new rice is cooked with milk and sugar (Kshiri) and then offered as Bhog to Goddess Laxmi. Then the eldest member of the family distributes the same to other members.

**Basanta Panchami:** The day marked for the propitiation of Saraswati, the Goddess of learning is known as Sripanchami or Basanta Panchami. The words 'Sree' and 'Basanta' are significant to the festival. 'Sree' is beauty and the other name of 'Saraswati' and Basanta is spring season which brings beauty and pleasure to the Earth. Therefore it is a festival to welcome beauty through worship of the Goddess.

The worship of Saraswati is prevalent since the age of the Vedas where she has been referred as Bacha. During the Puranic age the tradition became more established and she was adored with anumber of names. At this stage Her form was conceived and accordingly images were built. Clad in white, She rides a white swan while playing a veena. White is the sign of her purity. She is the Goddess of music, poetry, learning and eloquence, indeed, of all the arts and sciences.

In some scriptures Saraswati has been described as the wife of Brahma. But, the widely held view is that She was created by Brahma out of His own intuitive powers and therefore, She was His daughter. Vishnu is the preserver of the universe and for this job He needed both learning and intellect, and Goddess Saraswati fulfilled this need by becoming His wife. In Her four hands She holds a stylus, a book and plays a veena (flute) with two. The stylus and the book signify learning and the veena, music. She is seated on a lotus which signifies beauty and heavenly origin. The swan is the vehicle as of Her father Brahma.

In some scriptures she is also known as Brahmi, Bharati, Gira, Barnamatruka etc. In the Vedas the supreme deity of learning has also been referred to as Agni or fire. This lends credence to a significance that fire is the source of light and light is the source of knowledge. It was, therefore, natural to he early Aryans to propitiate the Goddess as Agni or fire.

This festival, held on the fifth day of the bright fortnight of the month of Magha is mostly celebrated in the educational institutions. Students observe fasting since morning, wear new garments and propitiate the Goddess to bestow them with learning and eloquence. They offer 'Puspanjali' (handful of flowers) to the deity and then break their fast. Images of the deity are built by traditional clay-modellers, who are famous in the country for their artistic skill. They make hundreds of such images small and big, for sale. In the evening cultural programmes and feasts are arranged as a part of the celebration. The next day, the images are taken in procession to nearby tanks or rivers for immersion.

**Hingula Yatra:** Most of the festivals prevalent among the low-caste Hindus are either associated with the worship of Shakti or Shiva It is believed to have grown out of the mass religious culture of the people under the spell of Tantrism in the remote past. One such festival is Hingula Yatra or Patua Yatra. There is a popular belief among the local people that on this day of Visuba Sankranti Goddess Hingula appears and propitiation to Her removes all evil forces. She is worshipped in the village street on Her imaginary stride to the village. Offering to Her includes spitted new cloth, Pana(sweet-water), butter lamp and green mangoes.

In remote villages this festival is observed with much austerity. Those who observe fasting, especially women are called 'Osati'. Prior to the day of worship the fasting worshippers (mostly men) move from village to village with the sacred-pitcher symbolising the Goddess. Their religious procession is always accompanied by singing and dancing.

These worshippers are called Patuas. The man who dances with the holy-pitcher on his head wears a black skirt, a red blouse and a long piece of black cloth tightly covering the head and having equal length on both sides to flow. While dancing, the Patua holds the ends of the cloth and moves them artistically with stretched arms in perfect harmony to the rhythmic pattern. Sometimes he dances on the stilts and performs difficult Yogasanas balancing on the head, the staff that holds the holy-pitcher (Ghata). A big brass bell played with a cane-stick provides various peculiar rhythms. Sometimes country drums are also played.

The head of the patuas is called Bada-Patua or Katha Patua. All the Patuas observe fasting on this day. In the afternoon they assemble near a tank or river where all the rituals take place. The priest performing the rites is always a non-brahmin known as 'Jadua' or 'Dehuri'. During the rituals men, women and children of the villages congregate The surrounding reverberates with auspicious 'Hulahuli' (a shrill sound made by wagging the tongue inside the mouth) and 'Hari Bol' cheers of men. Then, sharp iron hooks are pierced through the skins on the back of the Patuas. During this ceremony the morale of the Patuas are boosted through holy cheers of the onlookers and they themselves loudly continue singing in praise of Hingula or Mangala.

In some areas Jhamu Yatra is organised. Persons observing Brata or vow in honour of the deity walk on thorns and on the bed of live charcoal amidst holy cheers and loud drumming. Those who walk on fire are known as Nian Patua (Nian for fire) and those on thorns are called Kanta Patua (Kanta for thorn). Some worshippers stand on edged swords and are carried on open palanquins. They are caned Khanda Patua (Khanda for sword). Some of them show some feats in deep water. They are called Pani Patuas

(Pani for water). Especially all these festivals are celebrated a Shiva or Shakti Shrine. Therefore, scholars are of opinion that these rituals, of inflicting injury to the persons by the devotees are related to the Tantra culture. By doing these they try to draw the kind attention of the God or Goddess whom they seek to propitiate.

**Uda Parab:** In some areas especially in Mayurbhanj and Keonjhar districts of Odisha a flying festival popularly known as Uda Parab is observed. The participating devotees of this festival are called Bhokta or Bhakta. As in similar other festivals, almost all the devotees belong to the low-caste Hindus.

In a village field a long staff is fixed horizontally on a perpendicular pole. The Bhoktas, after having the ceremonial bath and other rituals in a nearby river, move dancing in a procession to this place accompanied by a cheering crowd and loud beating of drums. There a huge congregation enthusiastically awaits their arrival. Then, one by one, they are tied to the horizontal staff with a long cloth at the shoulders. Ankle-bells are fitted on their feet. Some devotees are not tied. They simply hold on the staff with one hand and move hanging. With the help of a rope fixed to the perpendicular staff they are moved round and round by a person below. Profusely garlanded, the Bhokta flying at a height throws flowers from his garlands and green mangoes to the audience below, who collect them with great enthusiasm as precious possessions. After this ceremony the Bhoktas go to the nearby temple and offer offerings and prayers to Shiva, Hingula, Mangala.

**Prathamashtami:** This is one of the most popular festivals of Odisha, peculiar to the region in which the eldest child of the family is honoured. He or she is given new clothes and is made to sit on a wooden pedestal (Pidha). In fornt of him/her an earthen pitcher, full of water is placed on handfuls of paddy. Above it a branch of mango leaves and a coconut is placed. Then, the mother or any other elderly lady wishes him /her long-life and good health by praying Sasthi Debi, the Goddess that protects children. The social significanc of this festival is that the first-borns are brighter and it is ultimately they who take up the burden of the family after the death of the parents. According to psychologists the first-borns are mostly healthy, obedient and tradition-bound. Therefore, the family tradition is maintained through them. For such obvious reasons the eldest child is honoured to occupy the respectable place in the family after the death of the parents. A special variety of cake is prepared on this occasion which is known as 'Enduri'. The cake is offered to the Goddess of Sasthi and then taken by all. In the temple of Lingaraj at Bhubaneswar, the festival is observed with great devotion. On this day the repesentative deity of Lingaraj is taken out in a palanquin to a tank called "Papanasini" which is situated just behind the temple.

**Baseli Puja:** Baseli Puja is also known as Chaiti Ghoda. In the month of Chaitra there is an exclusive festival for the bonafide fishermen community of Odisha who are popularly known as Keuta (Kaivatra). This festival is held for a full month beginning from Chaitra parba (Full moon of Chaitra in March) and ending with Baisakh Purnima (Full moon in April). During this festival Baseli, the horse-headed deity of the community is propitiated. She is considered to be the tutelar deity of the community. She may be considered as a form of Mother Goddess who was earlier formless. Later she took various forms according to the conception and needs of the various communities living all over the country.

By 5th-6th century A.D., worship of Shakti had gained tremendous prominence in Odisha. One of the four celebrated 'Peethas'(centres) of Buddhist Tantricism in India was located in Odisha. The Peethas had not only the support of a number of Sadhakas to go ahead with their spiritual pursuits but also gave an impetus to the people in general to appreciate the Tantric practices. Rigorous religious practices involved in the Tantric way of worship became wide-spread.

It is believed that this festival originated during 10-11th centuries when Hindu Tantra and Buddha Tantra merged into one. Baseli is one of the various deities of Tantra culture which evolved during this period. The horse-headed deity is seated on an earthern platform. She wears a blood-red cloth in her full feminine form. In temples and places of worship She is propitiated on each Saturdays and Tuesdays throughout the year. During the festival period where there are no such images; only the horse-head made out of wood is worshipped. Peculiarly the worshipping takes place in a house and that is Dhinkisala (the place where paddy is husked). It is because, the subsidiary profession of the community is to prepare and sell flattened rice(chuda).

Worship of Baseli or Basuli and the Dummy-horse dance inexplicably connected with its rituals and celebrations is the most important festival of the fishermen who observe it with great devotion and austerity. The details for the worship have been enunciated in 'Kaibarta Gupta Geeta' by Achyutananda Das, a mystic Oriya poet of 15th century A.D. Various legends prevail about the birth of the community and their tutelar deity and this particular text records one. According to this Geeta, when the world was in a deluge Vishnu Bhagwan could not find a place to rest.

So, He by His spiritual power reduced his form and rested on a floating Banyan leaf. As it was all the while dwindling on the stormy waves of the ocean He created a man out of the dirt of His ear-zone and asked him to hold the leaf still with the help of a row (kandiara). But, soon he fell into deep slumber. In the meantime a huge demoniac fish Raghab swallowed the man. Again the leaf began dwindling and God's sleep was disturbed To His utter surprise He found the man missing. By intuition He could know everything and at once killed the Raghaba and got the man out. Then God transformed the banyan leaf in to a horse. He summoned Biswakarma and asked him to build a boat immediately. Then He said to the man "Hence-forward you and your community will be known as Kaibarta and you would be the king among them. Go to the country of Simhala and rule there happily. Make this horse your carrier and use this boat for trading. As you were swallowed and almost got killed by a fish, generation by generation you would kill the species and live on them." Baseli, became the name of the horse and God asked the man to worship him as his tutelar deity on the full-moon day of Chaitra. Since then the tradition is followed. The Dasa king sailed to Simhala with the horse by boat. There he ruled for many years. The horse died at the age of one lakh years and out of his carcass came out a damsel as beautiful as Lakshmi. She approached the king and lamented that no longer the name of Baseli would be associated with her. Taken by surprise the king was terrified. He then prayed Vishnu for His counsel. The God again directed, "This woman will be known hence-forth as Aswini Baseli whom you would propitiate for generations. Then only you can attain Baikuntha". Since then the woman became Goddess Baseli with a horse-head and continued to be venerated by the fishing community. Another legend is associated with the worship of the horse-head and the horse-headed deity. It is said that after the death of Baseli, the sacred horse God distributed his limbs among fishermen, confectioners (Gudia), oil-merchants (Teli) and cobblers (Mochi). They continued to worship the limbs. Some time after an idea struck to them. All of them agreed to assemble the limbs and have the full form of the deity (horse) and worship him commonly. This was done. At one time the Kaibartas and the Gudias vied with each other. A communal riot ensued, Gudias being rich and powerful locked the deity in a house and deprived the Kaibartas from worship. The helpless Kaibartas simply prayed the deity with utmost devotion for His return. Moved by the prayers of the Kaivartas he crushed the wall with the force of his hoofs and escaped to their camp. Being enraged the Gudias chopped of his head and even then, the head lived to accept worship and offerings from the Kaivartas. It is, therefore, the Kaivartas who worship the horse-head separately.

Inexplicably connected with the festival is Dummy-horse dance of the community. On the auspicious day of Chaitra Purnami, the Kaibartas worship a Bamboo with vermillion, candle-paste, butter-lamp etc. Then the bamboo is split ceremonially into pieces out of which only twelve are taken out for preparation of the frame of the dummy-horse. The frame is dyed red with red clay and then covered with a Pata (indigenous silk cloth). Then a painted horse-head made out of wood is fixed to the frame. A garland of Mandara (Hibiscus) flowers is placed on the neck during worship. This particular garland is always intended for mother goddess. Thus the dummy-horse is worshipped till the eighth day of the dark fortnight after which it is taken out for dance. A man enters the cavity and hangs the frame on the shoulders and then dances to the rhythm of Dhol (country drum). Mahuri is the only wind-instrument played during the dance. Songs are sung intermittently in votive dedication to the deity. Sometimes the dancer gets possessed and falls in to trance. Then somebody else replaces him. Two other characters Chadhua-Chadhuani or Rauta-Rautani also sing and dance. The male character dances with a long staff in his hand symbolising the profession of fishermen's rowing of boats. The female character is played by a man. Both of them sing songs of love and daily household chores. Then a song combat ensues which lasts for the whole night. During this portion of the dance the dummy horse is ceremonially placed in the centre and the performance is held in front of it, people sitting all around. There are regular amateur as well as professional groups for this dance. They perform on payment. Sometimes they move dancing from door to door and collect money. There are five to seven persons in all in a group including dancers and musicians. They continue to dance till Baisakh Purnami when they make a grand finale and then part for the next season.

Now-a-days the votive dancers are not confined only to the Kaivarta community. Since the dummy-horse dance is attached to many Shakti shrines of Odisha also, people of other communities have also taken interest to join the votive dancers. The dummy-horse dance is mainly prevalent in the coastal districts of Cuttack and Puri. In Puri the dummy-horses are profusely decorated with flowers and the 'Tahia' (Archaic head-gear of flowers) presents a magnificent show during dance. When the festival ends the horse-head is taken out ceremonially from the frame and is preserved in a temple. Next year during the festival it is again brought out and repainted for worship and use during the dance.

**Janmashtami:** The birthday of Lord Krishna, the eighth incarnation of Lord Vishnu, is celebrated as Janmastami. It falls on the eighth day of the dark half of the month of Bhadraba. Of all the divine incarnations of the God, Sri Krishna is the most adored. By virtue of His divine Leelas or sports, Krishna has become the darling of the humanity. The purpose of taking this avatar or incarnation was, as explained in the Bhagavat Geeta, the annihilation of evil and the establishment of truth and virtue. As such, from His infancy onwards Krishna destroyed numerous demons (suggestive of evil forces) who were harassing the Gods and men alike. Later, as an ally of the pandavas, He brought about in the interest of truth and justice, the war of Kurukshetra to destroy the wicked Kauravas and restore legitimate rights to the honest and truthful Pandavas. It was from this battle field that He delivered His Message to the suffering humanity which has come down to us as the most sacred book 'Geeta'. All His sports or Leela have been elaborately described in the Bhagavata, Mahabharata, HariJanma and many other religious texts. The birth day of the Lord is, therefore, celebrated as one of the greatest of all Hindu festivals in all houses. Lord Krishna was born at mid-night when the moon entered the house of Vrisabha at the constellation of the star Rohini on the eighth day of the dark half of the month of Bhadrab. Therefore, it became customary to observe fasting upto mid-night till the exact hour of birth. When the fixed hour comes conches are blown, gongs are sounded, slogans involving the God are given which heralds the birth of Krishna. After this Bhog (food offering) is offered to the deity and the fast is broken. The festival is widely celebrated in all vaishnavite temples, monasteries and houses. Clay images of Krishna are also worshipped on this occasion. The festival is devoutly observed by the cowherd community of Odisha, as Krishna lived and spent his childhood days in Gopa. The next day is observed as 'Nandotshaba' by this particular community as a reminiscence of the festival that was held by Nanda Raja, to celebrate the birth and arrival of Krishna. The young boys sing songs related to Krishna's sport and dance to the beats of resonant sticks. While vaishnavism was the court-religion of Odisha since 11th century A.D., the cult of Krishna worship was made popular during 15th century A.D. by Shri. Chaitanya and his followers. Though temples exclusively dedicated to Krishna are few in Odisha, the representative deities at Lord Jagannath are no other than Krishna who is known as Madana Mohana, Ramakrishna, Gopala, Gopinath etc.

**Raja Sankranti:** Raja Sankranti (Swing festival) or Mithuna Sankranti is the first day of the month of Asara (June-July) from which the season of rains starts. It inaugurates and welcomes the agricultural year all over Odisha which marks, through biological symbolism, the moistening of the summer parched soil with the first showers of the monsoon, thus making it ready for productivity. To celebrate the advent of monsoon, the joyous festival is arranged for three days by the villagers. Though celebrated all over the state it is more enthusiastically observed in the districts of Cuttack, Puri and Balasore. The first day is called Pahili Raja (Prior Raja), second is Raja (Proper Raja) and third is Basi Raja (Past Raja). According to popular belief as women menstruate, which is a sing of fertility, so also Mother Earth menstruates. So all three days of the festival are considered to be the menstruating period of Mother Earth. During the festival all agricultural operations remain suspended. As in Hindu homes menstruating women remain secluded because of impurity and do not even touch anything and are given full rest, so also the Mother Earth is given full rest for three days for which all agricultural operations are stopped. Significantly, it is a festival of the unmarried girls, the potential mothers. They all observe the restrictions prescribed for a menstruating woman. The very first day, they rise before dawn, do their coiffeur, annoint their bodies with turmeric paste and oil and then take the purificatory bath in a river or tank. Peculiarly, bathing for the rest two days is prohibited. They don't walk bare-foot do not scratch the earth, do not grind, do not tear anything apart, do not cut and do not cook. During all the three consecutive days they are seen in the best of dresses and decorations, eating cakes and rich food at the houses of friends and relatives, spending long cheery hours, moving up and down on improvised swings, rending the village sky with their merry impromptu songs. The swings are of different varieties, such as Ram Doli, Charki Doli, Pata Doli, Dandi Doli etc. Songs specially meant for the festival speak of love, affection, respect, social behaviour and everything of social order that comes to the minds of the singers. Through anonymous and composed extempore, much of these songs, through shere beauty of diction and sentiment, have earned permanence and have gone to make the very substratum of Odisha's folk-poetry.

While girls thus scatter beauty, grace and music all around, moving up and down on the swings during the festival, young men give themselves to strenuous games and good food, on the eve of the onset of the monsoons which will not give them even a minute's respite for practically four months making them one with mud, slush and relentless showers, their spirits keep high with only the hopes of a good harvest. As all agricultural activities remain suspended and a joyous atmosphere pervades, the young men of the village keep themselves busy in various types of country games, the most favourite being kabadi. Competitions are also held between different groups of villages. All nights 'Yatra' performances or 'Gotipua' dances are arranged in prosperous villages where they can afford the professional groups. Plays and other kinds of entertainment are also arranged by enthusiastic amateurs. The special variety of cake prepared out of recipes like rice-powder, molasses, coconut, camphor, ghee etc. goes in the name of Poda Pitha (burnt cake). The size of the cake varies according to the number of family members. Cakes are also exchanged among relatives and friends. Young girls do not take rice during the three-day festival and sustain only with this type of cake, fried-rice(mudi) and vegetable curry.

**Chaitra Parba:** The 'Chaitra Parba' or 'Chhau Festival' commences from the 11th April every year and continues for three days concluding on 'Mahavisuba Sankranti Day' at Baripada. This is the festival of festivals which is enjoyed by the people of the country and the enthusiasts from abroad.

**Kartika Purnima:** The whole month of Kartika (October-November) is considered to be the most sacred among all the twelve months of the year. During this month all the pious Hindus refrain from eating fish, meat or egg. All of them take pre-dawn bath and visit temples as a matter of routine. The last five days are considetd more sacred in which there is wide participation. Taken together the days are called 'Panchaka', the last day being the Kartika Purnima. Every day they take food only once in the afternoon which is known as 'Habisha'. For all the five days the women after purificatory bath in the early morning draw beautiful flower-designs around the chaura (a small temple like structure with a Tulasi plant overhead) with colour powders produced indigenously. Fasting for the day is commonly observed. Most of the Shiva temples get crowded with devotees offering prayers to Lord Shiva who is said to have killed the demon Tripurasura on this day. Group-singing of kirtans and loud beating of Mrudanga and cymbals continue for the whole day. Another festival that takes place in the morning is significant to the ancient history of Odisha. This reminds the maritime glory of the State. In olden days the Sadhabas (Sea traders) used to sail off to distant islands like Java, Sumatra, Borneo, Ceylon etc. for their trade by huge boats (Boita). The women of the community were giving them a hearty send off on this day. The days are now gone, but the memory is still alive. Now, people float tiny boats made out of cork and coloured paper or bark of the banyan tree while reminiscing the past glory. This is called 'Boita Bandana'. The next fortnight of the month is spent propitiating the dead ancestors. In every evening, a covered but perforated earthen pot carrying an earthen lamp inside is hoisted to a pole to help guide the ancestral spirits to descend on their respective villages and homes. The members of a family light a bunch of jute-stalks with the invocation "Oh! the ancestors come in the darkness and go in the light." This is called 'Badabadua Paka'.

In the city of Cuttack and some other places huge images of Kartikeswar are built and worshipped. At night they are taken out in procession and are immersed in the river Mahanadi, near a Shiva temple. Exactly at this place a big fair known as 'Bali Yatra' is held for about three-four days. The name of the festival has two significances. Some are of opinion that on this day the Sadhabas were sailing off to Bali and therefore, the name. Some others believe that Sri Chaitanya the great vaishnavite saint of Bengal on his way to Puri landed on this day at Cuttack after crossing the sand-bed (Sand is Bali) of the river Mahanadi. Thousands of People congregate at the fair-ground where innumerable varieties of goods are bought and sold. People also enjoy boating with friends and family in the moon-lit night.

**Rama Navami:** The birthday of Lord Rama is observed as Ramanavami on the ninth day of the light half of the month of Chaitra. Though there are very few temples dedicated to Rama in Odisha, this festival is widely celebrated by the performances of Ram Leela (the sport of Rama) based on the famous epic Ramayana. Beginning from this day the performances continue for over a month. Some observe fasting on the day and take food only after visiting the temple. There are several centers where the performances are held with great sanctity. The Ram Leela, held in Asureswar of Cuttack district and Dasapalla of Puri district are well known. Deepavali: The quiet month of Kartika climaxes on the Deepavali night in the festival of lamps. It is the last day of the dark fortnight. This festival of lights is observed widely all over the country. In the evening all the homes are decorated and lighted with rows of earthen lamps. Varieties of crackers are also burst. Cakes and delicious dishes are prepared in every household. In all, the festival is celebrated with fire-works, illumination, feasting and gambling. The festival is also known as Kalipuja, as the Goddess is propitiated on this day. Huge images of the terrific Goddess are built and worshipped. This tradition has come to Odisha in imitation from Bengal. Some people, especially the business community observe it as a New Year's day and worship Goddess Lakshmi on the occasion. On this day they settle their business accounts, bury old enimity and start pursuits anew for the coming new year. Worshipping Lakshmi on the day specified for Kali is also significant. In some Puranas it has been stated that Lakshmi, the Goddess of wealth was a captive in the nether world. On this day she was freed by Vishnu form the clutches of Bali. Therefore, the festival is celebrated in Her honour. Another account is available which says that this day is the reminiscence of the festival that was held by the rejoicing people of Ayodhya to celebrate the coronation of Sri Ram. Therefore, the festival is marked with mirth and merriment. Peculiarly this festival is celebrated differently by the low-caste Hindus in the district of Mayurbhanj. They call it 'Bandana'. The festival is observed for three days beginning from Deepavali. On this occasion they worship the cows and bullocks. On the first clay the cattle are cleanly bathed in rivers or ponds. Then at home, their horns are oiled, their feet are washed with water mixed with turmeric and marks of vermillion paste are put on the forehead. In the afternoon sturdy young bullocks decorated with patches of colours all over the body and are tethered to poles with a strong rope. A group of people singing, dancing and playing drums (Madal) followed by an enthusiastic crowd approach the bullocks one by one. One of them holds tiger-skin and frightens the bullock. When the bullock gets terrified and charges violently, he gets away to the back or side foiling all attempts made by the bullock. Thus they make all the bullocks dance one by one tethered from one end to another in the village street. The nights are spent with drinking, feasting, singing and dancing. This reminds us of the bull-fight that takes place at Madrid in Spain.

**Khudurukuni Osha:** On the Sundays of the month of Bhadrab (Aug-Sept) this festival is observed by the unmarried girls of the business community of the coastal districts of Odisha. During the festival Goddess Durga is propitiated Khude Bhaja (Left out particles of rice that are fried), Kantiali Kakudi (Cucumber having little thorns on it), Lia (fried paddy), Ukhuda(fried paddy sweetened by molasses) and coconut are the food-offerings given to the deity. However, the principal food-offering is Khuda which is said to be the favourite of the Goddess. Therefore, the festival is named as "Khudarankuni" or popularly 'Khudurkuni' which means one who is very eager for khuda. In the early morning the girls go out collecting flowers required for the ritual. The varieties are Kaniara, Godibana, Tagara, Malati, Champa, Mandera and Kain. Then they go to nearby rivers and tanks to have purificatory bath. After this they build tiny temples of earth or sand and decorate the same with flowers. Paying obeisance to the deity there, they return to their respective homes. They take two and half mouthfuls of boiled rice mixed with water without adding salt. Then salt is added. The significance of this act is not known. After this the, whole day is spent in making garlands and decorating the image of the Goddess.

In villages generally the deity is worshipped in the Dhinkisala or the place where caddy is pounced. This place is plastered neatly with cow-dung and the image of the deity is installed. The floor is painted with floral despins known as Jhoti or Alpana. Garlands are made to hang like arches. The whole day passes with the arrangement and the rituals of worship commence in the evening.

After the ritual, are over the girls recite musically the episode of Taapoi which is now available in print. Eariler this was handed down by oral tradition. The first episode 'Malasri' recounts the killing of the demon by Durga. It is said, that Mahisasura, the terrible demon became atrocious by getting a boon from Brahma, the creator. Not only the mankind, but also the Gods got panicky. He became so powerful that even Gods couldn't kill him. Then all the Gods conferred and went to request the Goddess of power to kill the demon. Durga agreed and assuming the form of a beautiful damsel went to Vindhya mountain to pretend penancing. Mahisasura, while out on hunting, noticed the beautiful damsel and immediately offered to marry her. The damsel answered that she would only marry that person who would defeat her in duel. Mahisasura being confident of his power soon agreed to the proposal. A fierce 'duel' ensued between them; with all her enargy the damsel thrusted a trident violently to the chest of the demon who was killed. Thus, Durga redeemed the world from the fear and atrocity of the demon. It is, therefore, believed that the girls worship Durga to be powerful like Her, to fight evil forces for the goodof the human race.

The second episode 'Taapoi', is a legendary account of the sufferings and success of a Sadhab (Sea trader) girl. It also reminds us of the maritime glory of ancient Odisha, when there was sea-borne trade with south-east islands of Java, Bali, Sumatra etc. The Sadhabas of Odisha were a prosperous community who had trade-links with many countries. According to this tale, there were seven brothers in a prosperous Sadhaba family. Taapoi was their only sister who was also the youngest. Obviously they bestowed their love and affection on her lavishly. Whatever she wished immediately her demands were fulfilled. One day the little girl was playing with her friends with a winnow, made out of bamboo strips. A Brahmin widow of wicked nature scoffed at this. Being hurt the girl demanded a golden winnow to play and it was given. Again she demanded a moon of Gold. When it was half done her father died. When it was completed her mother died. By that time the family also became poor. The seven brothers then set out on their voyage to distant lands for trading and while leaving left clear instructions to their respective wives to take special care of their lovely sister. Soon after the brothers left the seven wives fell on the bad counsel of the Brahmin widow who impressed upon them that the cause of their poverty is the girl for whom they were so lavish. Soon they changed their attitude. She was not given good food or clothes. She was made to live on khuda (left out rice particles) and was engaged to watch goats in the jungle. Inspite of unbearable torture she waited patiently for her brothers to return. The youngest sister-in-law was kind to her, but couldn't come to her rescue because of the six others. Amidst all sufferings Taapoi held her morale high. All the while she was praying Durga (Mangala) for the safe return of her brothers. She worshipped the Goddess along with other girls and offered khuda as she had nothing else. Her sincere and devotional prayer yielded fruit and her brothers returned safely. They landed on the shore at night and while resting on the vessel they heard the wailing sound of a girl. Being curious as to who was crying they searched the area and found to their utter dismay, that she was none else than their dear sister. As the pet goat 'Gharamani' was missing, she was driven out by the in-laws and without being able to find the goat she was helplessly crying. Seeing her brothers, her joys knew no bounds. The brothers heard all about her plight at the hands of their wives. To punish them they asked their sister to cut their noses. But, their noses were restored when she again prayed the Goddess. Then all of them went happily home. These two episodes set two ideals before the girls who observe the festival. One is to be courageous like Durga to fight evil forces and the other to be like Taapoi to bear all sufferings patiently to come out successful in life. The idols of Durga are then immersed in rivers and tanks and this marks the closing of the festival. Savitri Brata: The Amavasya (last day of the dark fortnight) in the month of Jyestha is known as Savitri Amavasya or Savitri Brata. This day is most auspicious for the married Hindu women with husbands alive. They observe it as a vow with great devotion and pray for the long life of their husbands.

The Brata has been named after Savitri. In Mahabharata and other puranas the romantic episode of Savitri-Satvaban has been elaborately narrated with ideological veneration. Savitri was the beautiful daughter of king Aswapati of Madra Desa. She was unparallel both in virtue and beauty. As a suitable groom couldn't be found out, her father gave her complete freedom to choose her own partner in life. With a band of veteran ministers she travelled many countries and religious centres in search of a suitable partner, but couldn't find one of her choice. While returning desperately a handsome young man caught her eyes. He was engaged in cutting wood in a jungle. The young man was no other than Satyaban, a prince in exile who was living in the forest with his blind father Dyumatsen. Savitri selected him as her life's partner. But Narada forecasted that he would die young. Then the king asked his dear daughter to select another. But, Savitri was firm in her determination and ultimately married him. She left the palace and lived with her husband and the in-laws in the forest. As a devoted wife and daughter in-law she took all pains to take care of them.

Gradually the ordained time for the death of Satyaban drew near. One day while cutting wood in the jungle his head reeled and he fell down from the tree and then expired on the lap of his beloved wife, Savitri. Then appeared Yamraj, the death God to take away the soul of Satyaban from his body. Savitri, deeply hurt pleaded to Yamraj not to be separated from her husband. If at all he would take away the soul of her husband she would also follow. Yamraj was taken aback at such a request and explained that it was impossible.

Instead he wanted to grant three boons. Savitri cleverly asked for three boons and Yamraj, in haste, conceded to it. Savitri could regain the kingdom of her father-in-law by his first boon; get back the eyes of her in-laws by the second boon. The third boon was that she would be the mother of hundred sons and without a husband it was an impossibility. As a Sati, she can't take another husband. Yamraj, being out witted and moved by the devotion of Savitri returned the life of her husband. Satyaban came to life again and both of them lived happily thereafter.

In deep regards to Savitri all Hindu women observe this festival worshipping and propitiating her as a Devi. The morale of the festival is to teach the women to be virtous devotional and painstaking like Savitri to make worldly life happy and peaceful. In the early morning the women take purificatory bath and wear new clothes, new bangles and apply vermillion on the fore-head and the hair-parting line. Images of Savitri are never made. The grinding stone (sila-pua) is represented as Savitri and worshipped. Wet pulses and rice, mango, jackfruit, lemon, banana and several other fruits are offered as Bhoga (offering). After observing fasting for the whole day they simply take the Bhoga. In the afternoon when all formalities of worship are over they bow low to their respective husbands and elderly people.

**Dhanu Yatra:** Dhanu Yatra relating to the episode of Lord Krishna's visit to Mathura to witness the ceremony of 'Bow' organised by Kansa as described in the 'Bhagawat Purana' is colourfully observed at Baragarh in Sambalpur district. The entire topography of Baragarh is rendered into the elements of Drama. The town of Baragarh becomes Mathura, the river Jira becomes Yamuna and the village Amapalli on the other bank of the river becomes Gopa. Different acts of the Puranic description are performed at their right places and the spectators move from place to place with the actors to seethe performances. The drama and reality get inextricably fused. The festival continues for 7 to 11 days preceding Pausa Purnima, the full moon day of Pausa which falls in December-January every year. The performances are held from 3 P.M. to 9 P.M. which are followed by entertainment programmes during the whole night.

**Kumar Purnima:** Kumar Purnima is the full-moon day in the month of October-November. This autumn festival is one of the most popular and important festival of Odisha. Kumar or Kartikeya, the handsome Son of Shiva was born on this day. He also became the God of war. As young girls always wish for a handsome husband, they propitiate Kumara who was most handsome among the Gods. But, peculiarly enough there is no ritual for the God, instead the Sun and the Moon are worshipped.

In the early morning the girls after their purificatory bath wear new garments and make food-offerings to the Sun. They observe fasting for the day. In the evening when the moon rises they again make food offerings of a special variety and take it after the rituals are over.

It is a festival of rejoicing for the girls. All of them sing and dance. The songs are of special nature. They also play a kind of game known as 'Puchi'. They also indulge in other varieties of country-games. This day is also observed as the birth day of Lakshmi, the Goddess of wealth. Therefore, many people worship the Goddess at their homes and keep themselves awake by playing Pasha (Chess), and other indoor games. Significantly it suggests that those who wish to acquire wealth should always be vigilant at night. It is for this reason the owl, the bird which sleeps in the day and comes out only at night.

**Shamba Dasami:** The tenth day in the bright fortnight of the month of pousha (Nov.-Dec.) is known as Shamba Dasami. The day is dedicated to the worship of the Sun God and is peculiar to Odisha. There is a legend attached to the festival which tells about how and when the festival came to be observed. It also finds mention in the Shamba Purana. Shamba was the most handsome son of Krishna who was also very proud. He never paid any respect to his elders and mostly spent his life in licentious habits. Once he came across Narada, who is revered by all Gods and Goddesses. But Shamba didn't pay any respect to him. Instead he played tricks. This enraged the sage. In order to take revenge of this insult Narada made a false allegation against him before his father Lord Krishna that he had seen him in love-play with Gopis who are to be respected like mothers. Enraged with this Krishna cursed him to be afflicted with leprosy. As a result Shamba got afflicted with leprosy and lost his handsome features which were his pride. Narada never believed that the curse would be so severe. He repented and then advised Shamba to go to the Maitreya Bana to sit in penance to receive the blessings of the Sun God who would only cure him from this dreadful disease. Shamba sat in penance for long twelve years. Being pleased with his devotion the Sun God cured him of the disease. The day Shamba was freed from the disease is known as Shamba Dasami. The day is observed as a festival to propitiate the Sun God as the best healer of diseases.

Maitreya Bana is identified with the present site of

Konarak where Shamba spent the rest of his life worshipping the Sun God. Later, considering the religious importance of the place Langula Narasingha Deva, the mighty Ganga ruler of Odisha built the famous shrine of Sun God at Konarka in 13th century A.D.

This is another variant of the legend about Shambara Dasami. It says that once Narada came to Dwarka. There he found Rukmini the spouse of Krishna to be morose and tearful. On enquiry Rukmini disclosed that she gave birth to a child as beautiful as Madana, the Cupid, but he was abducted by a demon and since then there is no end to her plight. Then Narada consoled and advised her to pray Sun God to get back her child. To arouse belief and strength in her, he narrated another story about the efficacy of such prayer. This tale has it that there was a Brahmin in Arka Kshetra (Konarak) named Goutama. He had three beautiful sons by his wife Padmamukhi. To his ill luck all of them died one by one. His grief-stricken wife attempted to commit suicide. The Brahmin forbade her and then persuaded her to pray Sun God. She sat in deep penance praying the God. Being moved by her devotion and, prayer the Sun God fulfilled her desire and she was again blessed with children. Narrating the story Narada advised Rukmini to worship the Sun God accordingly. She followed his advise and prayed the God with utmost devotion. In the mean time, the lost child Pradyumna killed the demon Sambarasura who abducted him and came down to his parents in a Vimana (aircraft). Both Krishna and Rukmini became overjoyed getting back their son. According to this version, as the demon Sambarasura was killed on this day, the festival is known as Sambara Dasami. This festival is mostly observed by the elderly women who propitiate the Sun God to keep their children free from all diseases. Those who are childless also pray for children. On this day, the Sun God is invoked thrice. Once in the morning, then at mid-day and lastly in the evening, before the sun sets.

**Dola Purnima (Holi):** Dola Purnima or Holi is a popular festival in the coastal districts of Odisha. It is the full-moon day in the month of Falguna (March). Through the festival the spring is welcomed and enjoyed with mirth and merriment. This festival has been referred to in the puranical texts as Basantotsaba or the spring-festival. Some scriptures testify that the Madanotsaba, the festival held in honour of Madana or the Cupid was later transformed as the Dolatsaba or swing-festival of Krishna. Therefore, Krishna is propitiated on this occasion as Madanamohana. Description of the festival as Dolatsaba finds mention in a number of puranas and other Sanskrit texts. The Padma Purana says, "One is expiated of all sins, who gets a vision of Krishna swaying in the swing." Though the festival of Holi is observed for a day with mirth and merriment all over the country, the festival is celebrated for five days in Odisha. It starts from the tenth day of the bright fortnight of the month of Falguna (Feb-March) known as Fagu 'Dasami'. Smearing the heads with Abira (a violet coloured powder) the people take round the idols of Madanamohana in richly decorated palanquins known as Veemana. The procession is led by village drummers, pipers and the Sankirtana Mandalis. The procession halts in front of each household and the deity is offered Bhog. The daily rounds of the deity for the four days is called Chachery. On the final day of the purnima the celebration culminates in a swing-festival for the deities. The idols carried in veemanas from a number of villages assemble in an important place where swings are fixed on a platform. They are made to swing to the accompaniment of devotional music sung in chorus. In olden days the beginning of the new year vvas calculated from the spring-season. After the swinging festival of the deities, the Ganaka or Jyothisha (astronomer-cum-fortune teller) reads out the new Oriya almanac and narrates the important events that are to take place during the year. For this reason, some are of opinion that this festival is purely to celebrate the new year. On the fourteenth day of the fortnight there is a function in which a straw-hut is set to fire amidst much amusement and excitement. This is known as 'Holipoda' (burning of Holi). The legend about it is that, Holi was the most beautiful sister of Hiranyakashipu, the demon-king. As an ardent devotee of Shiva she got the boon that she would never die of drowning or burning. Inspite of all heinous attempts Hiranyakashipu couldn't kill his son Prahlada, the devotee of Vishnu Then he planned to burn him to ashes. As Holi would never get burnt she was asked to walk into the blazing fire with the child in her arms. Surprisingly the child came out unhurt but Holi was burnt to death. Enraged at this Hiranya asked Shiva about the inefficacy of His boon. Then Shiva replied, "I granted her the boon to protect herself, not to kill anybody." As a reminiscent to this, the Holipoda is celebrated and the next day is the festival of colours 'Holi', in which people smear colour powders on each other's face and head and squirt coloured waters. There is much fun and merriment in the festival. In some places the burning of the straw hut is known as Mendhapodi or the burning of a ram. A legend attached to it says that a demon known as Mesha was causing terror in the Heaven and Earth, Gods as well as human beings prayed Krishna to rescue them from his atrocities. Krishna killed and burnt him to ashes. It is, therefore to reminiscent this event that a hut is burnt which represents the abode of the demon. In many places of the State big fairs are arranged where idols of the deity are assembled. These fairs are called 'Melana'. The Veemanas of the surrounding villages are placed in a row for public view. Keen competition is observed in the decoration of the veemanas. When all the expected veemanas reach the place, display of fire-works takes place and this is watched by thousands of enthusiastic crowd. In the fairs agricultural implements, commodities, household articles and furniture are bought and sold. Such Melanas or Fairs continue till the month of Chaitra in different places of the district of Cuttack, Puri and Ganjam.

**Lakshmi Puja:** With the harvest brought home the farmers feel greatly satisfied with the yield. After six months of toil in the field, they fill the granaries with the blessings of Goddess Lakshmi. So, the whole month of margashira (Dec-January) is spent in worshipping the Goddess. All the rituals connected with the festival (Manabasa Gurubara or Lakshmi Puja) is done by house-wives themselves. On each Thursday of the month the houses are plastered with cow-dung, the floors are decorated with beautiful floral designs drawn with rice-powder mixed with water. This is called 'Jhoti'. Footmarks are painted from the doorstep to the place of worship as if Goddess Lakshmi has entered the house. The roofs are decorated with flower garlands and festoon woven out of paddy stalks. After purificatory bath in the morning the housewives worship the Goddess, not through an image but significantly through paddy-measures. Different varieties of rice-cakes and Kshiri (rice-soup prepared with milk and sugar) are prepared in every house hold and are offered to the deity and then taken by all.

In the evening the Laxmi Purana is read or recited in which an interesting story is told. Once Shreeya, an untouchable woman worshipped Goddess Lakshmi by observing this festival. Being moved by her devotion Lakshmi left Her permanent abode, the temple which is situated inside the campus of the temple of Lord Jagannath and visited Shreeya's house. When Lord Balabhadra, the elder brother of Lord Jagannath came to know about this, She was declared defiled and was not allowed to come back into the temple. Lakshmi was deeply hurt and went to her father Sahara.

When Lakshmi went out of the temple all wealth in the temple started vanishing. Later the Gods Balabhadra and Jagannath couldn't find food to sustain themselves. They came out of the temple in the guise of Brahmin beggars in search of food. Ultimately they landed at the door of the Goddess Lakshmi. Balabhadra apologised for the mistake and all of them returned to the temple. The Purana ultimately teaches all to pay extreme regard to Goddess Lakshmi and the person who disregards Her is sure to fall on evil days. This means that wealth should be well-protected and properly used and misutilisation of wealth is sure to make a person suffer.

**Sital Sasthi:** This particular festival strictly prevalent among the Brahmins of Odisha is generally observed in Brahmin villages, popularly known as Sasans or in towns where Brahmins are more in number. It is believed that Shiva or Hara became furious after Jagara Amavasya and He was cooled down only by marriage with Parvati. So, this marriage festival of Shiva and Parvati is called Sital (cool) Shasthi and is held on the sixth day of the bright fortnight of the month of Jyestha. Since the days of yore Odisha has been a seat of Shaivism. Bhubaneswar itself has about five hundred Shiva temples dating back from 6th-7th century A.D. In the early temples of Bharateswar and Parsurameswar there are elaborate scenes of Shiva's marriage with Parvati. It is therefore believed that this festival of Shiva's marriage is very ancient and is being carried down through centuries past.

In most Brahmin villages of Odisha there are temples of Shiva, Parvati and Vishnu. During this festival the elderly Brahmins of the village act as the parents of the bride (Parvati) and the bride-groom (Shiva) and all formalities of a Brahmin marriage are observed. In analogy with the society-marriages where somebody acts as a mediator, here, Vishnu, the God Himself takes the role. At first a proposal (written on palm-leaf) is sent from the bride's side to the bride-groom's father through Sevak who also carries Mahaprasad (Food offering of Lord Jagannath), coconut, betelnut, and a piece of new cloth as prevalent in marriage customs. With him goes a procession of torch-bearers, drummers and pipers. Thereafter, on the fifth day (Panchami) at past mid-night Parvati goes to the temple of Shiva in a procession where the marriage takes place with all vedic formalities. After the marriage is over a feast is arranged in which the Sevayats from both the sides participate. The real festival takes place next day in the night when the marriage procession is taken out with pomp and grandeur. The images of Parvati and Vishnu are carried in a richly decorated palanquin (vimana) heading the procession. Shiva, seated on a bull follows them on a bullock cart. At cross-roads and important places the procession halts and there is lavish display of fire-works, dancing, drumming and various other kinds of merry-making.

Though this festival is held in the temples of Loknath at Puri, Lingaraj at Bhubaneswar and in most of the important Brahmin villages, it is observed in a grand scale at Sambalpur where two groups of Brahmins exhibit rare enthusiasm to organise it with keen competitive spirit. During the procession lavishly decorated tableus are brought out. Traditional and local dance and music parties are engaged to move with the procession. Varieties of fire works are displayed. Each group tries its utmost to excel the other in every respect. The procession terminates at the respective temples and the festival ends.

On this day the town of Sambalpur wears a festive look. Thousands of people congregate from different parts of the district to witness the deities in procession. In the Puranas it has been said that one is expiated of all sins if he sees the Gods in procession. Therefore, there is a natural attraction for the common villagers to see the mounted deities in procession.

**Durga Puja:** Durga Puja (September-October) symbolizes the commemoration of good over evil. Life comes to a stand-still in the city of Cuttack as crowds pour over the Puja Mandaps to enjoy the festivities. On the day succeeding 'Vijaya Dasami', the last day of Dussera, the images are taken in a spectacular procession for immersion in the river Kathajodi.

**Magha Saptami:** This festival is celebrated on the seventh day of the new moon of Magha. This is a day specifically set aside for the worship of Sun God at Konark where stands the world famous Sun Temple, otherwise known as Black Pagoda, dedicated to Sun God. This is the most popular and colourful festival of the place when lakhs of pilgrims from different parts of India and enthusiastic visitors from abroad visit Konark to observe the festival. In fact this is the second biggest festival in Odisha, next to the Car Festival of Puri. The pilgrims take holy dips in the Chandrabhaga which meets here and welcome the rising Sun with prayers.

A big fair is held at the Khandagiri caves near for a period of seven days commencing from "Maghasaptami".

**Visuva Samkranti:** In India the months and years are counted on the basis of lunar or solar movements. According to the solar system the month is counted from Samkranti to Samkranti and in lunar system it is counted from Purnima (Full-moon) to Purnima. Visuva Samkranti is the first day of the month of Baisakh as well as the solar year. This is also called Mahavisuva Sankranti or Jala Visuva Samkranti In northern India it is called Jala Samkranti, in southern India Sakkar Pongal and in Odisha it is known as Pana Samkranti, named after Pana, the main drink offering specially prepared on this occasion.

There are specific reasons as to why the Visuva Samkranti is considered as the first day of the solar year. It is only on two occasions i.e. Mesha Samkranti and Tula Samkranti that the Sun fully rests on the equator and on these two dates the length of days and nights remain equal. After Mesha Samkranti the Sun moves in the northern direction to our side as our country is situated to the north of the equator. It is, therefore, from this day of first movement of the Sun from Mesha Samkranti that the new year is counted. All over the country this day is considered auspicious and is celebrated with social, cultural and religious performances.

In Bhabisya Purana, this festival has been mentioned as Jala Samkranti. According to tradition when Bhisma, the grand-father of Kurus and the Pandavas lay on the bed of arrows (Shara Sajya) he felt thirsty and there was no water nearby in the ravaged battle-field of Kurukshetra. Then Arjuna with his powerful bow thrusted an arrow deep into the ground and water immediately shooted out in a stream to quench the thirst of the dying warrior. Out of contentment and compassion Bhisma conferred to Judhisthira, "Those people who would offer cold water to thirsty people on this day would not only be free from all sins, but also the departed souls of their ancestors as well as the Gods in heaven would be pleased." This saying of the holy scripture is observed with great reverence and people all over the country offer sweet-water to thirsty people as a religious rite.

In Odisha, this festival is observed with great sanctity in various forms. On this day Chhatu (grinded corn powder), Pana (sweet water), umbrellas, fans (made out of palm-leaves or bamboo-strips) and Paduka (wooden slippers) are offered to Brahmins and the poor people. All these are the remedies for the scorching Sun. Water as the vital source of life becomes more symbolical in another ritual of the festival. Above the Tulasi plant- which is a must in every Hindu household of Odisha, a shed is prepared with branches of green leaves and painted pitcher of smaller size filled with water is suspended with a rope hanger. Beneath it a small piece of straw is fixed to a hole in the pitcher through which water is drained drop by drop on the Tulasi plant. This is called 'Basudhara' (the stream of the earth). Here, Tulasi plant symbolises the human life and it is to be saved from the scorching sun by resting in the shed and taking enough water.

This festival is observed widely in some form or other, in the coastal areas and in some towns and villages of other areas a rigorous ritualistic observance is observed. Deeply connected with the mass religious culture of Odisha, a number of other festivals otherwise known as Jhamu Yatra, Hingula Yatra or Patua Yatra, Danda Yatra, Uda Yatra etc. which originated as ritualistic observances of Chaitra Parva culminate in the Visuba Samkranti and make a grand finale of the whole celebration.

**Dusserah:** The holy scriptures testify that on this day Rama killed Ravana and his victory was celebrated. Therefore, it is also called 'Vijaya Dasami'. (Victorious tenth day). In Odisha it was, therefore, a military festival. In the villages the agriculturists worship their implements. The Khandayats or the Paikas bring out their rusty swords, spears and other weaponry to clean and worship. The Paika Akhadas are held in which young men indulge in stylised military dances, display of sword-fighting and various acrobatic stunts. People in general polish their instruments of profession at this time and also clean, plaster and whitewash their houses. Beautiful flower-designs are painted on both sides of the doors. Now-a-days idols of Durga are worshipped for five days, especially in towns and cities. This tradition of idol worship has been set by the Bengalis who dominated during the time of the British rule in Odisha. Especially in the city of Cuttack a large number of idols of Durga and Mahadev are worshipped in profusely decorated pandals. After Dasami all the idols are then taken in procession for immersion in the river Kathjori. Many people come to the city from villages to watch the festival.

**Shiva Ratri:** Every deity in the Hindu pantheon has a particular day dedicated to Him and that day is considered most sacred and auspicious to worship and propitiate. Jagara or Shiva Ratri or the night of Shiva is a festival held in honour of the God. In Shiva Purana, Shiva says to Her consort Parvati that no festival other than Shiva Ratri observed by his devotees gives Him so much pleasure and satisfaction. This festival is, therefore, observed with great sanctity by the people on the fourteenth day of the dark fortnight of Phalguna (February-March). In times of yore, Odisha was a great seat of Shaivism. It was the state religion for over four centuries and as a result, innumerable temples were built and dedicated to Shiva throughout the length and breadth of the State by the pious rulers. Bhubaneswar alone has about five hundred shrines for Shiva, both big and small. The earliest temlpes date back to 6th-7th century A.D. Since then Shaivism is a great religious force among the people of Odisha. Most of the prosperous villages have a temple for Shiva. Therefore, the festival is held with great religious fervor in the State. According to a legend it signifies the day on which Lord Shiva swallowed the deadly poison that emanated from the churning of the ocean of milk which would have killed the Gods. Not knowing that it would not cause any harm to Him, all the Gods and Goddesses kept vigil throughout the night praying for His life. The prayer that was offered to Him that night is repeated since then on Shiva Ratri. Yet another story tells that at the time of the deluge [Pralaya] the whole world was covered with utter darkness and the Divine Mother restored light to the world by offering prayer to Shiva. It is said that the rituals that are observed in the festival are the same as observed by the Mother Goddess. The devotees observe strict religious discipline by abstaining from food for the day and keep themselves awake the whole night. Shiva linga is worshipped with vilwa leaves throughout the night with chanting of the Panchakshyara mantra 'Om ! Namah Shivay !'. The next morning, they take their bath and after worshipping Shiva again break their fasts. Many are the stories narrated in the Puranas about the efficacy of the observance of this festival.The story of the king Chitrabhanu of Ikshvaku dynasty is one. It is stated that during his previous birth the king was a hunter by name Suswara and was eking out his livelihood by hunting birds and animals and selling them. On a Shiva Ratri day, he was roaming about in the forest and then shot a deer, but couldn't take his spoil home as he was overtaken by the darkness of the night. He got upon a vilwa tree and kept awake the whole night stricken with hunger and thirst. He had starved for the day and so couldn't sleep in the night due to hunger. While keeping himself awake for the whole night, he plucked leaves from the vilwa tree and dropped them one by one to the ground. He never knew that there was a Shiva Linga beneath the tree and the leaves he dropped fell on the Linga. When the day dawned he went home, sold the deer and purchased food for the family. He fed a stranger who begged him for food ,because of this virtuous deed that he performed, even if unknowingly, two messengers of Shiva came to him at the hour of his death and conducted his soul to the abode of Shiva. After enjoying divine bliss for long, he was again reborn as king Chitrabhanu of Jambudwipa i.e. India. According to another legend that finds mention in the Puranas, Brahma and Vishnu, the two supreme Gods had a difference as regards their supremacy. The matter was referred to Shiva for a verdict. Shiva, then asked both the Gods to gauge the depth and measure the height of his Linga. Vishnu took the form of a boar and dived below to ascertain the depth and Brahma on his swan vehicle scaled high to ascertain the height. High above in the void Brahma came across a petal of Ketaki flower drifting downwards. As it was falling from the top of the Linga, He asked the petal about the further distance upward. The petal couldn't answer since how many ages that it was drifting downwards. Brahma refrained from going up and went to the nether world to meet Vishnu. Showing the petal He claimed to have ascertained the height of the Linga. At this false pretext, the petal objected. As Brahma was exposed because of the disclosure of the petal, He, in wrath, cursed - "From this day you would be unworthy for the worship of Shiv". Vishnu, being pleased with her truthfulness blessed saying, 'On shiva chaturdaphi you will be worthy for Shiva's worship. Therefore only on this day Ketaki flower has the right to be offered to the deity. On no other occasion the flower is ever used for worship. Almost all the important shrines for Shiva bear festive look during the festival. Thousands of people flock to the temples from the early rooming to offer worship to the deity. In some places big fairs are arranged where large varieties of goods and implements are bought and sold.

**Viswakarma Puja:** Viswakarma is known as the divine engineer since the Puranic age. As a mark of reverence He is still worshipped specially by the engineering community. The festival is observed on the Kanya Sankranti Day (September) which follows the Ganesh Puja, in every industrial towns of Odisha. Towns like Hirakud and Rourkela present the grandest ceremony on the occasion depicting different fire works connected with modern technology. special festivals and events Kalinga Mahotsav 261 BC, the over ambitious Emperor Ashok invaded Kalinga and unleashed a bloody battle around Dhauli. The brave soldiers of the soil confronted the Magadhan army with unprecedented courage and patriotism. The war continued. One and half lakh were taken captive, one lakh were slain and as many as that number succumbed to the aftereffects. The war ended. Emperor Ashoka smiled and then laughed a hearty laugh, for he had won the war. But what came next was beyond his imagination. He found heaps of the dead, heard the wailing of the wounded and saw the tears rolling down the cheeks of those who suffered. The terrible massacre made him remorseful. He was gripped by a sense of guilt. He wished, he had not waged the war. He had conquered the territory but lost his way to come out of the agony. His victory echoed defeat from within. He became restless. At this juncture, appeared Upagupta, the Buddhist Monk and showed him the path of peace and non- violence. His face radiated with glow. His eyes brightened. Compassion permeated in him. He was rejuvenated with the Buddha's Vani. He realised the essence of conquest by Dharma in preference to the conquest by Force. He surrendered the sword and embraced Buddhism. History took a U-turn as he renounced the war for good. Kalinga showed the way from War to Peace like the lotus blooming from the mud. The message of peace and non-violence spread beyond the frontiers of India. Thus began a new era of art and education, peace and pilgrimage. To carry the message to the masses, he erected a set of rock edicts of which one is at Dhauli. He pronounced his reverence to all sects and tolerance to all practices. The earliest rock cut sculpture of India, the forepart of an elephant, was hewn out of live rock above the inscription. Dhauli came to be recognised as an important centre of Buddhist Heritage. There was also a Buddhist Monastery named Arghyaka Varatika existing here in 9th century AD. In 1972 the Kalinga Nippon Buddha Sangha built a Peace Pagoda, popularly known as Viswa Santi Stupa. Dhauli continued to be a living shrine of Buddhism in modern Odisha as well. The Dhabaleswar Siva Temple renovated in the same year in close proximity reaffirmed the sacredness of the site. On the outskirts of modern Bhubaneswar Dhauli emerges from the placid green countryside amidst a tranquil setting of paddy fields. The river Daya flows through little villages. A black topped road meanders from the high way to the Santi Stupa. Driving through the serpentine road smelling cheery odour of the cashew plantations is a pleasure. The hilltop provides a panoramic view of the Temple City of Bhubaneswar. The chanting of Buddhist hymns on one side and the Saiva stotra on the other purifies every soul. As a fitting tribute to the memorial of Dhauli and to commemorate the victory of Peace over War, a National Festival of Martial Dances was organised on 1st & 2nd February 2003. With the Viswa Shanti Stupa at the backdrop, eminent Dancers of India harmonised the vigour of martial art with the peaceable sublimity of dance tradition through scintillating performances representing Chhow and Paika from Odisha , Thang Ta from Manipur and Kalaripayattu from Kerala.

www.ingramcontent.com/pod-product-compliance
Lightning Source LLC
Chambersburg PA
CBHW031102080526
**44587CB00011B/784**